Men, Women and Equality

ISSUES FOR THE NINETIES

Volume 18

Editor

Craig Donnellan

Independence

Educational Publishers
Cambridge

First published by Independence
PO Box 295
Cambridge CB1 3XP

© Craig Donnellan 1996

British Library Cataloguing in Publication Data
Men, Women and Equality – (Issues for the Nineties Series)
I. Donnellan, Craig II. Series
305.3

ISBN 1 86168 001 5

Printed in Great Britain
at Leicester Printers Ltd
Leicester, Great Britain

Typeset by
Claire Boyd

Cover
The illustration on the front cover is by
Andrew Smith / Folio Collective.

CONTENTS

Introduction

Men, *Women and Equality* is the eighteenth volume in the series: **Issues For The Nineties**. The aim of this series is to offer up-to-date information about important issues in our world.

Men, *Women and Equality* looks at sex discrimination in the workplace and in education. The information comes from a wide variety of sources and includes:

Government reports and statistics
Newspaper reports and features
Magazine articles and surveys
Literature from lobby groups
and charitable organisations.

It is hoped that, as you read about the many aspects of the issues explored in this book, you will critically evaluate the information presented. It is important that you decide whether you are being presented with facts or opinions. Does the writer give a biased or an unbiased report? If an opinion is being expressed, do you agree with the writer?

Men, *Women and Equality* offers a useful starting-point for those who need convenient access to information about the many issues involved. However, it is only a starting-point. At the back of the book is a list of organisations which you may want to contact for further information.

*****

The Sex Discrimination Act

The Sex Discrimination Act 1975 makes it generally unlawful for an employer to discriminate directly or indirectly against women or men on grounds of sex or being married. References to a woman apply equally to a man.

Direct discrimination: where an employer treats a woman, on the ground of her sex, less favourably than he or she treats, or would treat, a man.

Examples
- Not interviewing or appointing a woman because it is felt that, because of her sex, she would not fit in.
- Sexual harassment of a woman at work.

There are only limited exceptions to the rule of no discrimination. These include where an employer seeks applicants for a job where being a woman, or a man, is a genuine occupational qualification for the job, for example where considerations of decency or privacy require the job to be held by a man or woman (e.g. a job as a changing room attendant).

Indirect discrimination: when an employer applies a requirement or condition equally to men and women, but a considerably smaller proportion of women than men can comply with it, and it cannot be justified as necessary for the job.

Examples
- Insisting on unnecessary height requirements.
- Requiring a person to be willing to work evenings when this is not operationally necessary.
- Automatically refusing training or promotion to part-timers if most part-time jobs are done by women but most full-timers are men.

Similar provisions relate to direct and indirect discrimination against a married person compared with an unmarried person.

The Equal Pay Act 1970

The Equal Pay Act requires equal pay for men and women doing the same sort of work or work of equal value for the same or linked employers. 'Pay' means any sort of remuneration, including pensions.

Like work

If a job done by a woman is the same as that done by a man, except that the man has very occasional extra duties, the woman can claim equal pay if she can show that the man's extra duties make no difference of practical importance.

Example
- A company employs female domestic cleaners who have the same duties as male labourers, except that the men have some additional duties such as sweeping leaves and snow. The women are paid less than the men. The women may have a claim to equal pay if the men's additional duties are seasonal tasks which make no practical difference to their usual run of duties.

Work of equal value

Even two very different jobs will have 'equal value' if they place on workers equal demands in terms of factors like effort, skill and decision. The employer must not give undue value to typically male qualities (like physical strength) at the expense of typically female qualities (like manual dexterity).

Example
- A female canteen cook was held by an industrial tribunal to be employed on work of equal value with that of male painters, thermal insulation engineers and joiners working for the same employer. The jobs were assessed under five headings: physical demands; environmental demands; planning and decision making; skills and knowledge; and responsibility. The overall scores of the jobs were found to be equal.
- The above is an extract from *Equality pays – How Equal Opportunities can benefit your business – A guide for small employers*. See page 39 for details.

© The Employment Department
January, 1996

Challenging inequalities between men and women

Information from the Equal Opportunities Commission

First among equals – through the glass ceiling

Women at the top

1972 First woman judge to sit at Old Bailey: Rose Heilbron QC

1973 First woman on London Stock Exchange: Susan Shaw

1975 First woman Lord Lieutenant: Lavinia, Duchess of Norfolk

1979 First woman Prime Minister: Margaret Thatcher

1979 First woman President of British Medical Association: Josephine Barnes

1983 First woman Lord Mayor of London: Dame Mary Donaldson

1984 First woman General Secretary of a big trade union: Brenda Dean, SOGAT

1984 First woman Law Commissioner: Brenda Hoggett

1992 First woman Speaker of the House of Commons: Betty Boothroyd

1992 First woman Director of the Crown Prosecution Service: Barbara Mills

1993 First woman Civil Service Commissioner: Ann Bowtell

1993 First woman head of MI5: Stella Rimmington

1995 First woman member of Bank of England's Court of Directors: Frances Heaton

1995 First woman Chief Constable: Pauline Clare, Lancashire Constabulary

1995 First woman executive director under 30 of a top company: Lisa Gordon, Chrysalis

First among equals – breaking new ground

Women into 'men's jobs'

1975 First woman jet airline captain: Yvonne Pope

1977 First woman firefighter: Mary Langdon

EQUAL OPPORTUNITIES COMMISSION

1979 First full time woman coastguard: Sue Nelson

1981 First woman station master: Pennie Bellas

1981 First black woman TV newscaster: Moira Stewart, BBC

1983 First woman train driver: Anne Winter

Equality in education

'76 Then . . .

Did you know that 20 years ago, many schools taught different subjects to girls and boys?

'96 Now . . .

The Sex Discrimination Act gave girls and boys the right to equal access to education. In 1989, the National Curriculum provided for all girls and boys to be taught the same subjects.

The last two decades have seen tremendous progress in closing the gap between boys and girls in education. Girls have caught up and are doing as well as boys in mathematics and science – which used to be thought of as 'boys' subjects'. Yet it takes a long time to change attitudes about what girls or boys can study at school and beyond. For example, girls still choose secretarial courses, while boys choose to train in areas like engineering and construction. However, women have made major inroads into the professions. Increasing numbers of women study medicine (one third of all doctors are women, as compared to one sixth in 1975), law (1 in 16 solicitors were women in 1975, as compared to nearly half now), architecture and accountancy. Men are also increasingly entering the traditional 'women's' professions of nursing and secretarial work.

Equality in retirement, health and caring

'76 Then . . .

Did you know

– that women were entitled to a state pension and free prescriptions at 60, but men had to wait to 65?

– that married women were invariably expected to care for an ill or elderly relative for nothing?

'96 Now . . .

Since 1995 men can get free prescriptions at the same age as women and the pension age will be equalised at 65 by 2020.

Since 1986 married women can claim Invalid Care Allowance to look after a relative at home.

Twenty years ago, if a married woman did not go out to work, she was expected to depend on her husband's pension or benefits in old age or ill health. Since then, more women get full state pensions in their own right. Women and men have the same right to most social security benefits. In April 1978 sex discrimination in access to company pension schemes was outlawed (before that date women did not have this right). And the pension age will soon be the same for women and men. Men have gained greater equality in free access at 60 to concessions like free swimming tickets and senior citizens' rail cards; and women have benefited from equal access to some benefits up to 65. But many part time workers still do not get a pension from their jobs. And most women remain poorer than men in their old age and have to rely on smaller state benefits.

There is still a lot of work to do before the role that women play in caring for children and elderly relatives is recognised in our state pensions and social security benefits. And the benefits system still discriminates against widowers who are bringing up children alone.

Sporting chances

'76 Then . . .
Twenty years ago, girls were not allowed to play rugby or football at school and women were not even allowed to play in official darts games.

'96 Now . . .
In 1995, for the first time, a girl, age 11, played Rugby League for her team at Wembley, and women competed equally with men for a place in the darts World Championships.

Two decades ago many sports were regarded as suitable only for boys. Sport is one of the areas in which long hard battles have been fought for greater equality between the sexes. Many schools now offer the full range of sports to girls and boys. Women now compete in almost all sports and take part increasingly in traditional 'men's' sports such as rugby and cricket. However, outside the education system many sporting activities are still open to young people of one sex only, and there are still male bastions which women have not breached, such as the pavilion at Lord's Cricket Ground. But the last five years have seen many firsts in sport for women.

First among equals – the games people play

1977 First woman to ride in the Grand National: Charlotte Brew on Barony Fort

1977 First woman football referee of all-male match: Jenny Bazeley

1992 After a five year battle, Susan Thompson becomes Britain's first ever woman professional pool player

1993 The first woman boxing Master of Ceremonies, Lisa Budd, settles her sex discrimination claim, with EOC support.

1994 First woman linesperson in football league match: Wendy Toms

1995 EOC helps Beverly Davis establish that she can stand for election to the National Executive Committee of the Rugby Football Union

1995 Sophie Cox granted permission from the Rugby League to play for Rochdale Town Under 11 Schools Team and played for her team at Wembley on 28 October.

Changes and challenges

In 1995, the EOC, the Northern Ireland EOC and the Women's National Commission, representing over 8 million women, jointly launched our National Agenda for Action, which sets out what still needs to be done to achieve lasting equality.

In a rapidly changing world, different attitudes and new laws have helped us move towards greater equality between women and men. But we still have a long way to go before everyone has an equal opportunity, regardless of their sex, to do what they want to do and be what they want to be. Equal opportunities are about allowing every individual to get the best start in life and to reach their full potential. The EOC will continue to help women and men who have been unfairly treated. We are here to work with employers, national and local government to change attitudes and remove discrimination. Our vision is for a better, more just society in the 21st century.

● The above is an extract from *Challenging inequalities between men and women*, a publication produced by the Equal Opportunities Commission.

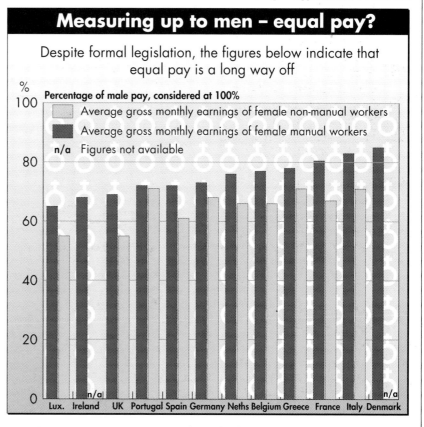

Measuring up to men – equal pay?

Despite formal legislation, the figures below indicate that equal pay is a long way off

%

Percentage of male pay, considered at 100%

☐ Average gross monthly earnings of female non-manual workers

■ Average gross monthly earnings of female manual workers

n/a Figures not available

100 · 80 · 60 · 40 · 20 · 0

Lux. Ireland UK Portugal Spain Germany Neths Belgium Greece France Italy Denmark

The long struggle for equality

The history of attitudes to women's work shows the slow progress of turning legal equality into real equal pay

The recent campaign to increase the representation of women in Parliament through all-women shortlists of Labour Party candidates in some constituencies caused much controversy. It was one attempt to give women more political power; another is the activity of those behind Emily's List – an organisation which provides financial support to women who want to become Labour MPs. Both initiatives are attempts to overcome the problems women face in gaining access to Parliament – in which no woman MP took a seat until 1919.

Both the role of women and the way in which work is organised have changed significantly over the past 200 years. Until the late 18th century, when most people in Britain lived in the countryside, the family was the main economic unit. Mothers, fathers and children worked together as a team in many occupations: on farms, in trades, even in mines. Most women worked from home where they could combine looking after the family with earning money – producing textiles and clothes, selling food from their kitchens, working at various crafts.

It was not until the industrial revolution in the mid-18th century that women started to do paid work outside the home in large numbers. The invention of new machinery changed people's working lives. New towns sprang up, along with fresh employment opportunities. By 1851 one third of all women worked outside the home. One of the biggest new employers was the textile industry. Most textile manufacturing moved from the home to the factory where it was done by machine. In 1851 it is estimated that it employed around 1.3 million people, half of them women. In the cotton industry in Lancashire, for example, women

WE'RE IN THIS TOGETHER!

worked as combers, carders and weavers. But in some towns they were excluded from jobs such as spinning and supervising, which were better paid.

Women were also employed in metal trades such as ironworks. They also worked in the printing industry, and they continued to work in mining.

It was common for the newer industries of the 19th century to contract out tasks to workers in workshops or at home. Known as out-workers, they worked in the industries that had sprung up in each area.

In Birmingham in the mid-19th century women made nails and chains in sheds attached to their houses. In Nottingham women made lace at home. But conditions were notoriously bad and the workers' pay extremely low. As a result, these occupations came to be known as the 'sweated trades'.

Up until the first world war the most common type of employment for working-class girls was in domestic service. Many girls travelled hundreds of miles to find jobs The work was hard and poorly paid, with an average housemaid's day being from 6am to 10pm. It was preferred by many to factory work, however, as it was regarded as more respectable for girls.

However, 'suitable' work was also being found in the offices of the expanding commercial and financial sectors. The new skills of shorthand and typing were deemed suitable for women but not after they were married. In most occupations, including teaching and shop work, which were also seen as appropriate for women, the common practice was to sack female employees once they were married.

The 'domestic ideology' – the idea that women's and men's worlds were separate, and that men should go out to work to support their families while their wives stayed at home – grew up in the late 18th century among the new middle classes. But the reality was that most poor women had to work.

Another problem was that many men saw women workers as a threat to their own jobs and status. Some trade and crafts banned women from membership and were therefore able to restrict the type of jobs women could get, pushing them into lower-paid work. Women were also barred from most professions until 1919 and the Sex Disqualification (Removal) Act.

Middle- and upper-class women at this time were not expected to go out to work. While most accepted this, some rebelled. Elizabeth Garrett (1836-1917 struggled to become the first qualified woman doctor in Britain in 1870, while Mary Somerville, who was the daughter of an admiral, became a renowned scientist. Many women from more affluent families campaigned actively for the vote for women in the suffragette movement at the end of the 19th century, and went to prison for their beliefs.

With the onset of the first world war, women had the opportunity to take on jobs they had never been allowed to do before. As the men went off to fight, there was a tremendous need for extra labour. In 1917 Woolwich Arsenal – where munitions were made – employed 28,000 women. When the war ended, though, there was a national campaign to persuade women back into the home as wartime industries had become redundant. By 1918 women were successful in gaining the vote; this was seen as a 'reward' for their hard work during the war.

Similarly, during world war two women were called back into the labour force, this time also working in the services. But once the war was over, they were again expected to return home as the labour market contracted; and many preferred to do so.

The economy has changed greatly since the last war. We are now in what is sometimes called the 'post-industrial' era, where heavy industries, which have traditionally employed men, are in decline, and services, where women's employment is concentrated, are expanding. Women now make up an increasing proportion of the workforce, and their contribution to the economy is huge.

However, the legacy of centuries old attitudes means that, although women are now winning higher-paid professional jobs, they are still, as in Parliament, in the minority.

Mary Macarthur (1880-1920)

Mary Macarthur was a central figure in the early women's labour movement. After working for her father she became president of the Scottish section of the Shop Assistants' Union. Many women were excluded from trades unions at the time, so in 1906 she helped launch the National Federation of Women Workers. By 1916 it had 60,000 members. Her campaigning led to minimum wage rates in some industries.

Work: progress on equality but still lagging over pay

By David Fletcher

Women are still under-represented in the ranks of power, policy and decision making, says a recent UN report, despite making big strides towards equality at work.

They are making inroads into some traditionally male professions such as the law, where women solicitors aged 30 and under now outnumber men. One in three practising solicitors is a woman, compared with only one in eight 10 years earlier.

Three-quarters of clerks and secretaries are women and women's careers still suffer more than those of men as they take time off to look after their children.

Though some women are among the higher salary earners, most are in lower paid work and fail to gain the same number of promotions as men.

Only three in 10 secondary school heads and deputies, for example, are women, even though almost half of secondary teachers are female.

Women outnumber men by four to one in the National Health Service but, says the report, 'they tend to be found in the less senior posts'.

At all ages, women earn less than men. 'The tendency for women to work in low-status, low-paid jobs is, of course, reflected in their earnings,' says the report.

One-third of women earn £190 a week or less, compared with 13 per cent of men. By contrast, three-quarters of men earn more than £230 a week, compared with only half of women.

Women earn more than their partners in only 13 per cent of couples.

Men and women received equal amounts of job-related training but their motivations are different: women want training to make their job more interesting, men seek it to improve the chances of promotion.

Asking for it

Imagine if, every year on International Women's Day, the Government passed a law especially for the benefit of women. In such a fantasy world, what would women ask for? We went onto the streets to find out . . .

Body and soul

'God, where to begin. Well, maybe making self-defence groups available to all women. They should learn how to defend their own space, not only physically, as in against attackers in the dark, but I think they should also have extensive education in assertiveness training. That's one area where women are really short-changing themselves.'   *Sofia, 21*

'Women have so much on their plate nowadays; they're running the house and they're out earning money. I'd like to give women more leisure time to do the things that they want.'
Joyce, 59

'Give them more freedom.'
Gilda, 35

'Make it so that every woman who suffered with cancer could get treatment straightaway on the NHS.'
Catherine, 52

'Let them all have a make-up session.'
Heather, 57

'I'd abolish the tax on tampons. In fact, I think I'd abolish payment on them altogether and make them freely available on the NHS.'
Chris, 50

Compiled by Kate Finnigan, Bronwen Roscoe and Lucy Williams

'Well, I'd make tampons free for a start, obviously, and then, I think I'd make manufacturers include free lacy panties in the packs of Super Plus. You know, for when you ruin your good keks and you have a hot date.'
Louise, 22

'Like some contraception, I would make tampons and sanitary products free on the NHS or at the Family Planning Clinic.'
Amanda, 32

'I would take luxury tax off feminine hygiene products. I think it's a real cheek that the Government are making money out of something that women have no choice over.'
Zoe, 24

Working it out

'Get rid of the Government and get more women into higher places. And maybe I would pass a law that protected women's job security if they became pregnant.'
Mrs Fernyhough, 58

'Bigger pensions for women.'
Mrs Murphy, 67

'More paid holiday.'
Justine, 27

'I would want more accessible, better public housing.'
Stacey, 24

'Try and make sure that women have equal wages.'
Una, 45

'Provide more childcare for women who work.'
Katherine, 25

'I would have equal pay in employment, as women are equally good at doing the jobs that men do and also have equally good qualifications. It just seems unfair to me.' *Bunty, 56*

'Provide tax relief for childcare.'
Helen, 42

'I would like to see better provisions made for childcare for working women.'   *Laura, 34*

'I'd make childcare provisions for working women free, or make it a big tax incentive for companies to start up crèches.'
Daphne, 38

'Working mothers still get a raw deal. If I were the prime minister I would make sure the Government paid for childcare.'   *Mary, 51*

'I would enforce crèche facilities in every work place, in order to bring us up to European standards.'
Marianne, 30

'Payment for women who stay at home to look after the children or for the men who do, and better career breaks for women who have children.'
Jenny, 45

'Get paid for your full maternity leave.'   *Elaine, 30*

THEY FOUND THAT ALL THE WOMEN IN THE WORLD HAD THE SAME FANTASY AND SO DECIDED TO DO SOMETHING ABOUT IT

'More pay when you're on maternity leave.'
Mandy, 27

'I would try to encourage women to learn not to compete with each other so much. Especially in the work place.'
Carmel, 31

'I'd make sure schools trained girls to be assertive right from the very first day. Girls always have a confidence problem. They have to know they are just as good as – and usually better than – men.'
Karen, 28

'True equality at work.'
Anne, 53

'Equal pay for women.'
Maureen, 56

'I'd probably make it so that there were more women bosses.'
Beverley, 21

'Enforce a law making prostitution legal. This would give prostitutes the right of protection under a union plus the recognition and acknowledgement received by any other company providing a service.'
Justine, 25

Man overboard

'Make it easier for women to have children and work and have a good life . . . actually, make men have children.'
Sally, 30

'Get rid of men.'
Nicole, 27

'I think men should have to wear skirts, it should be introduced as a sort of experiment, everyone should have to do it for a while. I think it's something that men deserve.'
Sarah, 25

'Abolish men.'
Kas, 32

'I'd insist that men have more sex education. So they know what to do!'
Rachel, 24

'If it were possible, I would change it so that men could have children, as I feel this biological difference is fundamental to why women get treated as second class citizens in society.'
Ginny, 26

'For me, it would have to be that women could stay fertile as long as men. This causes fundamental differences between the genders and one that causes farther-reaching repercussions for women in society – most of which are bad.'
Sally, 34

Back to basics

'I would encourage more girls to do sciences at school. I want to do civil engineering at university and I've just been to a university open day and I was the only girl there.'
Jennifer, 18

'I'd give women opportunities in education.'
Jane, 29

'The Government should make state nursery places available for all children so mums could be free to go back to work if they want.'
Becky, 36

'I would educate women about feminism and try to get rid of the stigma that is attached to it.'
Emma, 25

Play fair

'Get more women into Parliament.'
Justine, 27

'I would change the law, so that if a husband kills his wife it would be treated as murder, as is the case when a wife kills her husband. As it stands, this offence (when a husband kills his wife) is not taken seriously and therefore is more excusable.'
Louise, 31

'I would have more severe penalties for men who rape and violently attack women. I would also make sure that the police and the courts were more understanding and sympathetic towards women who have been raped, in order to ensure that more rapes get reported and less rapists get away with it.'
Jane, 40

'I would make sure that there was greater financial support for single parents. £6.30 per child, per week, is just not good enough – and the Government are going to cut that! It's impossible to find work when you can't afford a baby-sitter. I also feel that fathers should be penalised more if they refuse to give financial support.'
Stella, 34

© *Everywoman*
March, 1996

Cases brought under the Sex Discrimination Act in Great Britain 1989-1994

NUMBER AND PER CENT

Year	Total cases	ACAS[1] settled	Withdrawn	Successful at hearing	Dismissed	Disposed of otherwise
1993-4	1,969	824 (42%)	632 (31%)	176 (9%)	285 (15%)	52 (3%)
1992-3	1,386	504 (36%)	438 (32%)	127 (9%)	242 (18%)	75 (5%)
1991-2	1,104	378 (34%)	427 (39%)	90 (8%)	178 (16%)	31 (3%)
1990-1	1,078	335 (31%)	424 (39%)	78 (7%)	220 (21%)	21 (2%)
1989-90	1,046	384 (37%)	370 (35%)	86 (8%)	194 (19%)	12 (1%)

[1] Advisory, Conciliation and Arbitration Service (ACAS)

Source: Central Office of Industrial Tribunals

Official: men finally losing the sex war

By Rajeev Syal

The battle of the sexes has been reversed. For the first time, more men than women are claiming sexual discrimination in the search for jobs.

New figures to be published by the Equal Opportunities Commission (EOC) next month will reveal that more than half the complaints it received from job applicants last year were from men. A total of 820 alleged that potential employers had discriminated against them because they were male, compared with 803 complaints from women.

The shift is blamed by experts on the decline in traditional 'male' jobs in manufacturing industries. Kamlesh Bahl, chairwoman of the EOC, said: 'This is a significant departure. Men are facing discrimination when they attempt to move into jobs and professions traditionally held by women. It is a reflection of a radically transformed job sector.'

Complaints by men rose 10% on the previous year's figures, with record numbers suing for compensation over the past two years.

Typical is Brian Calder, 31, an east London bricklayer who retrained as a secretary. He was turned down for a job as a personal assistant last August after being interviewed by Terry Walters, his potential boss at a mobile phone retailer.

'Walters told me, "I want someone who is not going to want my job or moan if I ask them to make a cup of tea, so I am going to employ a woman". I was flabbergasted,' said Calder, who received undisclosed compensation.

Men also claim to have been excluded because male bosses believe an attractive woman is more appealing to customers. Piers Russell, 40, who was working as a receptionist at the Knoll Country Club in Corfe Mullen, Dorset, lost his job when it was taken over by a new company. All the staff were re-employed except for Russell. 'I was told by the new managing director that he intended to staff the reception with young girls and that I just wasn't as pretty,' he said. He won £3,405 compensation.

'The world has changed and it is men who are at a disadvantage'

Last week Vadivel Venkatasamy, 50, accused the Ministry of Defence of sex discrimination after it had rejected his application for a nursing post at Wellington Barracks in central London in favour of a woman. The ministry has agreed to review its recruitment procedures and paid him £2,500.

At the same time as men have been forced to seek lower-paid work in the service sector, they have also faced increasing competition for jobs as more women go out to work. While male unemployment stands at 10.5%, women have prospered with only 4.3% unemployed.

Experts said the EOC findings meant traditional feminist thinking should be reappraised. Camille Paglia, the American author, said: 'The women's movement has been in a fantasy world by advocating positive discrimination in jobs, while men have failed to get on.'

Neil Lyndon, the author of books critical of traditional feminist thought, said: 'This confirms what many have known for a long time. The world has changed and it is men who are at a disadvantage.'

Others, however, warned that many women were still underpaid compared with men. Lorna Russell, editor of *Everywoman* magazine, said: 'It is not a bad thing that men are starting to experience the low-paid jobs that women have had to do for years.'

© *The Sunday Times*
May, 1996

Women and men at work

CREW, an independent information and research centre based in Brussels, presents key points from *The Employment Report 1995*

For the past 20 years women 'have accounted for the entire growth' of the EU's workforce and 'are likely to continue to do so in future years'. The future 'productive potential' of member states' economies, said the report, 'is linked, to a major extent, to the skill levels of women.' For this reason, 'as well as for reasons of equity,' it is important that women have 'equal access to education and initial training and to continuing training throughout their working careers.'

Unemployment rates remain higher for women than for men even if they have similar educational levels. In 1994, 14.5% of women with no qualification beyond schooling were unemployed and just over 7.5% of those with a university degree or the equivalent. The comparable figures for men were 12% and under 5.5%.

The number of working women has steadily increased throughout the European Union over the past 30 years. From 1965 to 1975, their numbers increased by 3 million, or 7% of the active population, and by a further 10% from 1975 to 1985. By comparison, from 1965 to 1975, the number of working men fell by one million and from 1975 to 1985 by 3 million, or 4%. Only between 1987 and 1990, years of high job growth, was the decline in male unemployment halted and the number of men in work went up by 4.5%.

During the 1980s (1987-1990), women took up 55% of the net additional jobs created throughout the Union compared to 45% for men. The increase in men's participation was largely due to the high growth rate of industrial jobs during this period. One third of the new jobs created in industry during this period went to women. Women also gained 'disproportionately' from the

expansion in services during this period, according to the report. Women took 75% of the net additional jobs created over this period in the services sector 'much more than their share of employment' (under half in 1987). In agriculture, which continued to shed jobs between 1987 and 1990, the rate of job losses for women and men was equal (around 10%).

Since 1990, women's employment has only fallen slightly while male employment has resumed its downward turn. Men lost some 4.5 million (or 5%) jobs between 1990 and 1994, more than cancelling out the gains they had made during the previous three years of employment growth. Job losses in industry (down 12%) between 1990 and 1994 accounted for this downward trend in male employment.

During 1990-1994, there was a continued expansion of women's employment in services sector (by 1.5% a year, some four times the rate of growth of jobs for men in the sector). But this was not sufficient, unlike in the past, to compensate for job losses by women in industry and agriculture.

Despite the greater job losses suffered by men, the unemployment rate is higher for women than for men in all member states except the

UK, Sweden and Finland. The report explains this by pointing to the 'substantial increase in the number of women' entering the labour market 'which has outstripped the expansion of jobs.' Unemployment has fallen slightly more for men than for women since the second quarter of 1994 when it reached its all time high of 11.4%. In May 1994, the average unemployment rate for women stood at 13.1% of the working age population compared to 10.4% for men whereas in 1995 these figures were 12.8% and 9.8% respectively. The report predicts that this trend will continue for the next year or so 'as manufacturing output and jobs begin to recover and as increasing numbers of women are attracted back into the labour force by the prospect of employment opportunities.'

During 1990-1994 'the lack of job opportunities seems to have persuaded a significant proportion of men in particular either to withdraw from the labour force or to delay entry. At the same time, the upward trend in the proportion of working age women looking to work, which has persisted at a relatively high rate throughout the 1980s, slowed appreciably. These developments had a marked effect in preventing unemployment from rising even more than it did during this period.' This phenomenon has important implications for the future, the report warns. If many are attracted back into the workforce as more jobs become available, this will result in only a slight reduction in unemployment despite employment growth.

● The above is an extract from *The Employment Report 1995*, which appeared in CREW Reports Vol 15 No 11/12 Nov/Dec 1995. See page 39 for address details. ©*CREW 1995*

A time for women

Patricia Morgan gives three cheers for the market economy as it creates new jobs for women, but warns that it's bad news for men – and families

Those who first framed equal opportunity legislation could not have foreseen the extent to which the monumental structure of male livelihoods which resulted from the industrial revolution would be swept away. Had they known, would they have acted differently?

The data speak for themselves. There are now only 250,000 fewer women with jobs than men. Male wages, especially at the bottom end of the market, have stagnated or declined as women's wages have risen. The laws of supply and demand ensure that men cannot command the sort of rates they enjoyed when they monopolised the labour market.

The new pattern of short-term or part-time work is traditionally associated with married women, who move in and out of the workforce in response to family requirements. In the past, such jobs used to supplement a main wage; but women are now the primary source of income in as many as 30 per cent of households.

While equality activists still rage at 'dominant ideologies' that 'sustain male employment', the support which men, young ones especially, are able to offer families, has been dramatically reduced by levels of job insecurity unprecedented since the industrial revolution.

Men's diminishing ability to provide for families has contributed to the high numbers of casual unions and fatherless children on both sides of the Atlantic. The decline of the male breadwinner also accounts for both the increased inequality of family incomes since the late 1970s and the surge in child poverty. The proportion of children under five whose parents receive either income support or family credit – which supplements the net income of those in low-paid employment – stands at around 40 per cent. Among those with children aged between 12 and 15, the figure is 30 per cent.

In the first half of this century, women's participation in the workforce was concentrated in the years before marriage. The postponement of childbirth, and the growing availability of jobs in the new health and educational sectors, are the main causes of the increase in the number of married female workers which began in the 1960s.

Any reduction in women's workplace efforts is seen as a waste of 'human capital'

If the Government has any employment policy today, it is the drive towards equality in the workplace. This has been adopted at a time when the Government has

abandoned the goal of full employment – once the basis for its family support programmes (enshrined in the Beveridge package of the early 1940s). Today, taxation on families has exacerbated the effects of equality in the workplace on a couple's capacity to support a family.

Over the past few decades, the rate of taxation on families with dependent children has increased far faster than taxation on singles, and families with one main earner have borne a disproportionate share of the burden. A family man is now left with only £4.97 a week more than a bachelor after income tax, and chancellors have been urged to phase out the remaining fiscal recognition for marriage. This, argue the reformers, would help further undermine patriarchal assumptions about men's financial responsibility for families – considered by feminists to be at the root of the disadvantage which women have experienced in the labour market.

The two-income norm, based on equality of the sexes in the workplace, makes child-rearing an expensive use of women's time. The higher a woman's earnings at marriage, the older she will be at the time of the birth of her first child, and the smaller her family will be – if she has one at all.

Dual-career couples have become the yardstick. The 'market family' is served up as the model for *all* couples, and used to evaluate the experience of *all* working women. Its conception of equality is rooted in the career aspirations of bourgeois women, driven by an ethos of self-development and power.

But, in practice, dual careers make it difficult for couples to co-operate effectively. Even if fathers increase their share of household tasks, each parent has to put in more hours. The price for two full-time workers in terms of fatigue, conflict and overload, is immense.

There is still a strong preference in favour of the family as the rearer of children. When people are asked to choose what work arrangements they think best for families with children, nearly 80 per cent opt for the mother being at home until the children reach the age of five. Only 3 per cent opt for two full-time jobs. As children grow older, the preference shifts to part-time work for the mother. Many mothers are already coping with work patterns they regret: around two-thirds of dual-income families want a parent at home.

Prior to the 1960s few feminists downgraded child rearing or opposed the family. Feminists did not only advocate the entry of women into the professions and politics, they also wanted measures to foster the special contribution of mothers – arguing that, if mothers had to support families financially, this would amount to a further, unfair burden. Women's occupational advance and the protection of the family had to be reconciled: the entry into the market of hard-pressed secondary earners was in nobody's interests. When, in 1924, Eleanor Rathbone called for equal pay and an end to sex discrimination in employment, she insisted that families be compensated for the loss of the man's 'living wage' through the establishment of child and home-maker allowances.

Today, escape from home is, it seems, in everyone's best interests. From Barnardo's to the Adam Smith Institute and the National Children's Bureau, all agree that parental care must be superseded by specialised child-rearing institutions. It is assumed that a mother is only out of the labour force or working part-time because of the lack of child care. All *want* to work, *need* to work and *must* work, given the falling birthrate, rising male economic inactivity and earlier retirement. Any reduction in women's workplace efforts is seen as a waste of 'human capital'. Any expenditure on getting mothers to work, promises to pay for itself by providing a stream

---

Male wages, especially at the bottom end of the market, have stagnated or declined as women's wages have risen

---

of tax and insurance contributions for the Government.

Inseparable from these demands to complete women's 'marketisation' is the assumption that only achievement at work can determine status and fulfilment. Modern feminism, which sees the family as the source of subordination and inequality, has brought about a curious synthesis of Marxism and free market ideology. As people can no longer depend on family or community networks, the care these used to provide has entered the cash economy.

The truth is that huge amounts of unpaid labour necessarily underpin industrial economies. The social infrastructure created by domestic work would involve very significant

---

investment if it had to be provided by nurseries, counselling, hospitals, health centres, canteens, policing and so on. But there are limits on the ability of state institutions or market agencies to provide human care, if budgets are not to break and people are to thrive.

The family's early attachments are the basis of human culture, and child-rearing lies at the heart of the relationships, obligations and responsibilities which allow societies to function. The market and the state are also sustained and subsidised by moral economy. Both trade off social capital they cannot generate.

Many take a sombre view of the way in which global capital is now given free rein to destroy the social fabric, as the support which once sustained family and civic institutions is withdrawn. But others cheer on, as the market economy scoops up female labour. Women's time has come at last.

● Patricia Morgan is author of *Farewell to the Family?* (IEA). A longer version of this article appeared in the May issue of *Prospect*.

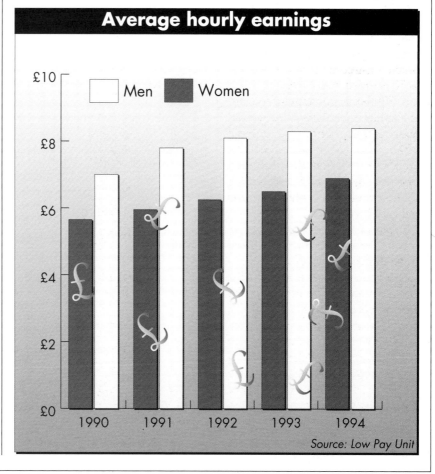

Average hourly earnings

Men Women

Source: Low Pay Unit

Wage determination and sex segregation in the labour market

Segregation by gender in employment 'is a pervasive and persistent characteristic of European labour markets,' according to a European Commission publication *Wage Determination and Sex Segregation in Employment in the European Community*.

The authors, Jill Rubery and Colette Fagan, both members of the Network of Experts on the Situation of Women in the Labour Market, looked at institutional arrangements, pay structures and labour regulations throughout the European Union for their impact on women's employment.

The report shows that social attitudes and values have a major impact on pay differentials between women and men. Women have a significantly higher risk of being low paid than men, according to the report, which said that EU figures show that women are 1.5 to 2.6 times more likely to be low paid than men. With the exception of Belgium, one-fifth or more of full-time women employees are low paid (that is, receive less than two thirds of average earnings) and the authors said the proportion would be higher if part-time workers were included. Women account for between 49% and 82% of low paid workers in member states.

The authors emphasised that women's work is not just underpaid, it is undervalued. Those who care for people, mainly women, are at a disadvantage when it comes to making a living. They emphasise that this undervaluation is not the result of a large supply of service-providers compared to service-demanders, as economic theory suggests. It is mainly the result of the fact that women's caring role within the home remains unwaged and unrecognised.

The various minimum wage systems in operation in Europe are examined and the report confirms the prevalence of women in several low-pay sectors. Their analysis of female-dominated job sectors suggests that the existence of a generalised minimum wage in a country is preferable to several industry-based minima.

In their examination of collective bargaining mechanisms across Europe, the authors found that women are overrepresented in sectors falling outside collective bargaining structures while they are under-represented in sectors where higher minimum wage rates are set and in those where collective bargaining improves on the pay and perks of industry-wide agreements.

Women's underrepresentation in trade union hierarchies is seen as contributing to the ineffectiveness of collective bargaining in improving women's positions. In conclusion, the authors state that collective bargaining cannot solve the problem of low-paid female-dominated job sectors. The authors consider that full-employment strategies are the most effective way of securing the economic rights of women.

The authors propose three angles from which gendered wage gaps can be tackled:
– fairer payment regimes and pay levels by facilitating judicial equal pay claims
– monitoring and promoting the advancement of the equal pay principle
– gender-proofing all labour market policies by governments and organisations.

● *Social Europe: Wage Determination and Sex Segregation in Employment in the European Community*, published by the European Commission's Employment and Social Affairs Directorate (DG V) in its Social Europe series, is at once analytically rigorous and accessible to non-economists.
Available from the Office for Official Publications of the European Communities, L–2985 Luxembourg or from government publications sales offices in member states.

© CREW Reports 1995

Countries ranked by share of low paid workforce	% of workers in full-time employment receiving less than 66% of median wage		% of women among low-paid full-time workers[1]
	all workers	female workers	
Belgium	5	10	62
Netherlands	11	28	53
Portugal	12	19	49
Germany	13	33	82
France	14	20	51
Italy	14.5	23	62
Ireland	18	29	51
Spain[2]	19	29	70
United Kingdom	20	41	63
Greece[3]	na	26	55

The extent of low pay and the concentration of women among the low paid in the EC

[1] Workers receiving less than 66% of median wage.
[2] Less than 40% of the median wage. Also includes domestic workers who receive benefits in kind.
[3] No estimate available for total share of labour force that is low paid, so Greece is not included in the ranking. As with Spain, the estimates include domestic workers, and also part-timers, but part-timers are only a small proportion of the Greek labour force.

Source: 'Social Europe: Wage Determination and Sex Segregation in Employment in the European Community

The inequality gap

From the Equal Opportunities Commission

Equal pay

Twenty years after the Equal Pay Act was passed, women still earn only 79% of men's full-time hourly earnings. They cluster in 'women's jobs' often undervalued and under-paid. Women are also the bulk of part-time workers with low pay and few opportunities for overtime or bonus earnings. Fragmentation of pay bargaining is likely to widen the gap, as is abolition of the remaining Wages Councils. Performance pay systems contain bias and leave a clouded picture that affects not only pay, but also training and promotion chances.

Britain introduced regulations in 1984 to provide for equal pay for work of equal value. But their complexity and limitations and the legal marathons they have launched, have meant they have had little or no effect on the inequality gap. The equal pay laws and administrative provisions are failing to provide justice and to ensure the principle of equal pay.

- Women in full-time manual occupations earn 63.4% of men's average weekly earnings. Women in full-time non-manual occu-pations earn 64.1% of men's average weekly earnings
- 76% of clerical and secretarial employees are women. 13% of employees in craft and related occupations are women
- The weekly average earnings of full-time women manual employees in hairdressing is £127.7p, and 10% earned less than £94.3p.

The EOC Equality Agenda for pay is:
- Government commitment to narrow the pay gap, tackling root causes revealed in research studies
- adoption of the Commission's proposals for amending the law and introduction of institutional protection for the lowest paid
- measures to change perceptions of the value of 'women's work'
- pro rata treatment and valuation of part-time work
- the integration of non-discriminatory pay determination and assessment by employers into their equal treatment policies, assisted by the Code of Practice on pay the EOC is now preparing
- policies to help both men and women reconcile the demands of work and family.

The above is an extract from *The Inequality Gap*, published by the Equal Opportunities Commission.

© Equal Opportunities Commission

Decline in the 1990s

The total number of MPs in the world (single and lower chambers) is 34,306, of whom, 3,737, or 11%, are women. This proportion is influenced by the higher rates in some countries with large parliaments, such as China's with its total membership of nearly 3,000. When rates instead of numbers are tallied, the world average slips to 9%. There are still a few countries – including Bahrain, Kuwait, and the United Arab Emirates – where women can neither stand for election nor vote. Women have recently been elected to parliament for the first time in Jordan (1 woman out of 80 MPs) and Morrocco (2 out of 333).

One step backward
Women as a percentage of parliamentarians worldwide

Slow steps forward
Percentage of women in senior management positions, United Nations Secretariat, 1949-1993

Source: United Nations, *Human Resources Management: report of the Secretary-General,* 17 October 1994.

Women's lot is still less pay, more work

Women in the 1990s: *Guardian* reporters look at a survey which says role of females has not changed much in a generation

By Chris Mihill

Modern women make up a larger section of the work-force but men are still paid more and do less of the housework, according to a detailed statistical portrait which shows that while much has changed, in many areas a woman's lot is much the same as her mother's.

They have fewer children and they have those later. More hold mortgages in their own right, and are happier doing a bit of DIY or gardening rather than knitting. But women are still the financial losers when partnerships break down, more have responsibilities as carers, and on average they have half the gross income of men.

More children are being born to older women, more women are choosing not to have children at all – and the birth rate is falling so that it is not sufficient to keep the UK population at present levels.

The report, *Social Focus on Women*, is drawn from numerous government demographic and economic surveys and was compiled for the UN conference on women in Beijing.

There were almost 24 million women aged over 16 in the UK in 1993, a 16 per cent increase on 1961. This is mainly accounted for by an increase in elderly women, with those aged 85 and over accounting for 3 per cent of all women, which will rise to 5 per cent by 2031. In terms of life expectancy a girl born in 1993 can expect to live to the age of 79.

In terms of household chores, women still tend to prepare the evening meal, do the washing and ironing, and cleaning, while men are responsible for household repairs.

There has been a slight nod in the direction of 'New Man'. The percentage of men who washed the evening dishes increased from 17 per cent in 1983 to 28 per cent in 1991 – but they were still much less likely than their partners to do other household tasks.

The number of families with dependent children headed by a lone mother nearly trebled from 7 per cent in 1971 to 20 per cent in 1993/94. Two-fifths were divorced. If separation occurs, nearly half of, women saw their income fall, as compared with a fifth of men.

The report says 12 million women work, over half of all women. Just over a quarter are working full-time. The proportion of working women rose from 44 per cent in 1971 to 53 per cent in 1994 and is predicted to increase to 57 per cent by the year 2006.

In both manual and non-manual occupations women earn less than men. In April last year, a third of women earned a gross weekly wage of £190 or less, compared with 13 per cent of men. In only 13 per cent of couples does a woman earn £50 more than her partner.

Although women dominate some sectors they are not attaining the top jobs. Women represent 81 per cent of teachers in nursery and primary schools, but only 57 per cent of head teachers. In secondary schools women represent 49 per cent of all teachers, but only 30 per cent of heads.

However, women are making inroads into some traditionally male preserves. There are now more women than men solicitors aged under 30.

The report paints a picture of women uninterested in politics with only 3 per cent being members of a political party, but active in church and voluntary groups, although membership of the Women's Institute and the Townswomen's Guild is declining.

One in six belong to a religious group or church.

The most common leisure activities for women are watching television or visiting friends, but the number gardening or carrying out DIY has increased since 1983, while those doing needlework and knitting has declined.

● *Social Focus on Women*, Central Statistical Office, HMSO. £25.

© *The Guardian*
August, 1995

Employment and key facts on women

From the Department for Education and Employment

Employment

(Unless otherwise stated, figures are taken from the most recent Labour Force Survey information, including the 'Rapid Release' where appropriate. This update includes data up to Winter 1995/96. Figures are for GB, men and women aged 16 and over and are not seasonally adjusted unless otherwise stated.)

Women in the labour force

- 12.3 million women are economically active
- 45% of people in employment are women
- The number of self-employed women has risen by 81% since 1981 (Seasonally adjusted)
- Women account for almost 1 in 4 of the self-employed
- Married women were 12% of the labour force in 1951*, about 25% in 1981* and around 30% in Autumn 1995
  * Population Census

Enterprise

- The number of women self-employed has risen by 81% since 1981. In Autumn 1995 seasonally adjusted, 792,000 women were self-employed (24% of total self-employment).
- In Autumn 1995, of all self-employed women 23% had employees.

Working patterns

- 82% of part-timers and 56% of temporary employees are women. 45% of women employees work part-time and 7% of men employees work part-time.
- 79% of women employees who work part-time say they do not want a full-time job. (Autumn 1995)
- The proportion of men in employment who are not full-time permanent employees has risen from 18% in 1981 to 29% in Autumn 1995; among women it has remained at about 50%.
- 4% of women in employment worked from home in Autumn 1995.

Earnings*

- Women's average hourly earnings (excluding overtime) were 79.6% of men's in April 1995. Women's average weekly earnings were 72% of men's weekly earnings. Women work, on average, a shorter week than men – with less overtime hours.

*Full-time employees on adult rates – pay not affected by absence. *New Earnings Survey: April 1995*

Industrial and occupational distribution of women in employment

*a. Industrial *(Autumn 1995)*
85% of all female employees, 91% of female part-time employees and 80%

of female full-time employees are in service sectors of industrial divisions. 18% (14% male) of full-time employees are in banking, finance and insurance etc. 16% (15% male) are in distribution, hotels and restaurants. 47% (30% male) are in 'other services' including transport, communication, public administration and health.

b. Occupational
25% of women work in clerical and secretarial occupations. 31% in managerial and professional (about 33% of whom are employed in associated professional and technical occupations as, for example, health associate professionals [e.g. nurses] or scientific technicians or social welfare associate professionals).

15% in personal and protective service occupations such as catering, domestic service and hairdressing and 12% in sales (winter 1995/96). 29% of all women working full-time are in clerical occupations compared to 20% of those working part-time (Autumn 1995).

International comparisons

- In 1994 the UK had the second highest female participation rate in the EU (Denmark had the highest).*
- 66% of women between 15-64 were in the labour market. There are more women in employment in the UK than in any other EU country, except Germany.
- Only Finland[1], Sweden[1] and UK[1] (EU) have a lower unemployment rate (international standard definition) for women than for men.

* *EC Labour Force Survey 1994*
[1] *Eurostat December 1995*

© Department for Education and Employment
May, 1996

Cases brought under the Equal Pay Act in Great Britain 1989-1994

Number and per cent

Year	Total cases	Withdrawn	Successful at hearing	Dismissed	Disposed of otherwise
1993-4	780	685 (88%)	19 (2%)	24 (3%)	2 (1%)
1992-3	240	83 (35%)	21 (9%)	34 (13%)	– –
1991-2	227	100 (44%)	5 (2%)	76 (33%)	1 (1%)
1990-1	508	246 (48%)	10 (2%)	25 (5%)	163 (32%)
1989-90	397	210 (53%)	33 (8%)	22 (6%)	68 (17%)

Source: Central Office of Industrial Tribunals

What is sexual harassment?

From the Equal Opportunities Commission

The EC code defines sexual harassment as:

'unwanted conduct of a sexual nature, or other conduct based on sex affecting the dignity of women and men at work. This can include unwelcome physical, verbal or non-verbal conduct'.

This definition is referred to in the Employment Department Guide for Employers, *Sexual Harassment in the Workplace*. The guide also refers to the EOC's Code of Practice which recommends that employers establish proper standards of conduct and behaviour in their organisations, and also take particular care in dealing with allegation of sexual harassment. The Trades Union Congress has defined it as

'unwanted verbal or sexual advances, sexually explicit derogatory statements or sexually discriminating remarks made by someone in the workforce which are offensive to the worker involved, which cause the worker

EQUAL OPPORTUNITIES COMMISSION

to feel threatened, humiliated, patronised or harassed, or which interfere with the worker's job security or create a threatening or intimidating work environment'.

(TUC Guide: *Sexual Harassment at Work*).

These definitions cover behaviour such as:
- comments about the way a woman looks
- lewd remarks or glances
- questions about a woman's sex life
- requests for sexual favours
- intimate physical contact
- sexual assault

Sexual assault by a colleague can also be a form of sexual harassment; women who have been assaulted should seek professional legal advice as soon as possible, and, report the incident to the police. A woman who feels daunted by the prospect of going to the police could take a friend or relative along with her, for moral support.

It is not necessary for there to a series of incidents; if one incident is sufficiently serious act it can constitute sexual harassment.

- The above is an extract from *Consider the cost . . . Sexual Harassment at work*, published by the Equal Opportunities Comission. See page 39 for address details.

© *Equal Opportunities Commission*

What can you do if you are sexually harassed?

From the Equal Opportunities Commission

Many women feel distressed and confused after an incident. Often they are made to feel that they are in some way to blame for it or they are led to believe that this sort of behaviour is normal or 'just a bit of fun'. Perhaps you have told a colleague who shrugs it off and tells you not to take things so seriously. Remember, other people's views don't matter. The important thing is how you feel about it. Ask yourself the following questions: Was the approach unwanted? Did it make you feel uncomfortable, intimidated, patronised or degraded? Was this linked to the fact that you are a woman?

Don't wait to be harassed out of your job. If you feel that you are being sexually harassed there are a number of steps you can take to deal with it. You have the right not to be harassed and you should not feel, or be made to feel, guilty or embarrassed about exercising your rights.

Your employers have a responsibility to take steps to prevent sexual harassment and to respond effectively to any allegation that is made.

You should take the following action:

Make it clear to the harasser that you object to his behaviour

You should ask the harasser to stop what he is doing. You may want to take a colleague or trade union representative with you. He or she will give you moral support. They will be able also, should the need arise, to give supporting evidence to an industrial tribunal. If you are too embarrassed to confront the harasser yourself, you could ask someone else to do it – a trade union representative, a trusted colleague, or a personnel officer might be willing to speak informally to the person on your behalf.

If you don't want to face the harasser, you might feel able to write to him. Write a letter or memo explaining what it is about his behaviour that is upsetting you, and ask him to stop. You could also say that you regard the behaviour as a form of sexual harassment and that if it does not stop, you will take further action. If you decide to tackle the problem by writing to the harasser, you should keep a copy of the letter or memo. You may need to show this to your employers, or an industrial tribunal.

Keep a record of the incidents

This is important. You will need to recall what has happened to you. Make a note of the date and time of any incidents, and of the name of anyone who was around at the time and might have seen what happened.

Report the harasser to someone in authority

You should do this even though you have made it clear to him that his behaviour is unacceptable. You should do this at the earliest possible opportunity. You may not be the only woman being harassed, but in any event, if your employers don't know what is going on they can't deal with the problem.

If a colleague is harassing you, go to your boss. If your manager or supervisor is harassing you, go to someone higher up, as well as to your personnel officer, and your trade union representative. If your local officer is unhelpful, get in touch with a National Officer or with the Women's Officer. You'll find the address and telephone number of the Scottish Trades Union Congress on page 39 of this book.

If the person harassing you is the owner, and you have no one in

the workplace to turn to, seek outside help. You will be able to get support and legal advice from a number of organisations. You could contact your local Citizens' Advice Bureau (CAB). Citizens' Advice Scotland will be able to give you the name and address of your local CAB. You may live near a law centre. The Scottish Association of Law Centres will be able to send you a list of law centres in Scotland. (You can obtain their telephone number by calling directory enquiries). You can of course get help from us at the Equal Opportunities Commission.

If necessary, seek medical help

If the nature of the harassment is such that it is putting you under stress, or injuring you, or making you unwell, go to your doctor. Apart from the medical help that your doctor can provide, he or she will also be able to give evidence at an industrial tribunal that you sought their help, and that you were distressed.

Follow up the complaint

Regardless of whether or not your employers have an agreed procedure for dealing with allegations of sexual harassment, whoever you have reported the problem to should make sure that your complaint is investigated quickly, that it is treated confidentially, and that the appropriate action is taken. Ask how your complaint is going to be investigated, and ask to be informed of the outcome. Make a note of the reaction to your complaint, and of any meetings or hearings that you have to go to. Remember that both you and the harasser will want to be represented at these meetings, so find someone to go with you.

Make a further report, if necessary

If the sexual harassment stops and you are satisfied with this outcome you don't need to do anything else. However, if you want an apology, or some other recognition of what has happened, or if the harasser then begins a campaign against you, for example by ignoring you, by passing your work to others, or by picking on you for minor mistakes, then report this as well.

Discreetly seek help from colleagues

Discuss the problem discreetly with colleagues whom you can trust. Some of them may have experienced a similar problem. You will feel better if you know you are not alone. Their evidence may also help you if you decide to go to an industrial tribunal. If any of your colleagues is also being harassed, ask her to keep a record too.

Ask your employers to introduce a policy

If your employers don't have a policy on sexual harassment, you might like to suggest that they adopt one as a preventative measure. Your employers can get advice about this from the Employment Service, ACAS or the Equal Opportunities Commission. The address and telephone number of ACAS can be found on page 39 of this book. The address and telephone number of your local Employment Service Office can be found in your telephone directory.

Remember that the person harassing you has a right to a fair hearing. Your employers will want to talk to the harasser. They may also want to speak to other people who might have been around at the time.

They will also want to treat your complaint as confidential. If your employers decide that your complaint is well-founded, they should discipline the harasser. They will want to do this in a way that accords with existing disciplinary procedures which, depending on the nature of the harassment, may result in the harasser receiving a disciplinary warning, or being dismissed.

If your employers decide that your complaint is well-founded but take no action against the harasser, you may have an additional complaint against them, either of sex discrimination or victimisation. If you find yourself in this situation, seek advice from the Equal Opportunities Commission.

● The above is an extract from *Sexual Harassment – how to deal with it*, a briefing produced by the Equal Opportunities Commission. See page 39 for address details.

© Equal Opportunities Commission

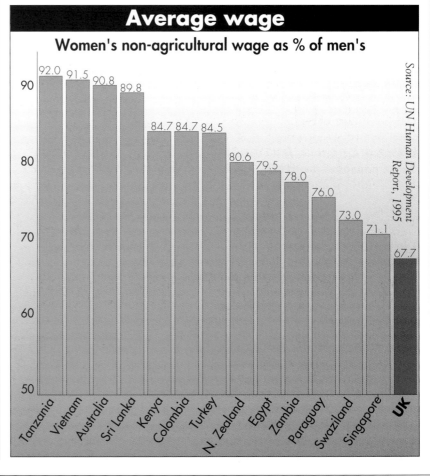

Average wage
Women's non-agricultural wage as % of men's

Tanzania 92.0, Vietnam 91.5, Australia 90.8, Sri Lanka 89.8, Kenya 84.7, Colombia 84.7, Turkey 84.5, N. Zealand 80.6, Egypt 79.5, Zambia 78.0, Paraguay 76.0, Swaziland 73.0, Singapore 71.1, UK 67.7

Source: UN Human Development Report, 1995

Sexual harassment cases in Scotland

From the Equal Opportunities Commission

The following are examples of sexual harassment cases brought before industrial tribunals in Scotland in which the applicants obtained compensation as a result of the behaviour suffered and the failure of the employer to take steps to end it. The names of the cases have been changed, but the facts are real.

Case One: A Regional Council v Smith

Mrs Smith was a laboratory technician employed by A Regional Council in one of their schools. She claimed that she was being sexually harassed as part of a deliberate and sustained campaign by two male technicians to persuade her to leave the school. The behaviour included making lewd suggestions and using phallic objects. Mrs Smith was compared with pictures of nude women in newspapers. One of the men often brushed himself against her. As a result of this behaviour, Mrs Smith sought to be transferred to another school.

The Court of Session in Edinburgh found that Mrs Smith had been subjected to less favourable treatment on the ground of her sex. It found that if any material part of the treatment included elements of a sexual nature to which a woman was vulnerable, but a man would not be, then this amounted to less favourable treatment.

Mrs Smith was awarded £3,000.

Case Two: MacDonald v A Timber Merchant

Ms MacDonald was working part-time with A Timber Merchant. After she was offered a full-time post, she was sexually harassed by a director. He made sexual advances to her which she rejected. When she informed him that she was going to take legal action for the sexual

harassment, he withdrew the offer of full-time work.

The Industrial Tribunal in Glasgow found that she had suffered sex discrimination by sexual harassment. The Industrial Tribunal found that she had been victimised by the director when he had withdrawn the offer of full-time work after she announced her intentions to seek outside help.

She was awarded £1,000 for injury to feelings.

Case Three: Jones v A Turkey Processing Factory

Mrs Jones claimed that she had been sexually harassed by the lewd behaviour of several of her male colleagues. She was employed as a butcher in a turkey processing factory and was used to swearing. However, an incident in which a colleague hung a turkey neck in the area of his private parts and one in which a song was sung which included rude words were offensive to her. She also found offensive references to menstruation and masturbation. She complained to her manager about the episodes and explained that she had been greatly upset by them. The employers told her that the language had to be viewed in the context of a factory where language standards were different from those in other settings. They also stated that there was evidence of dirty stories being told about which she had not complained.

The Industrial Tribunal in Edinburgh, however, found that she had been sexually harassed. It accepted that some dirty stories were told to which Mrs Jones had not taken exception, but was satisfied that she had found these four particular incidents offensive and had made this clear to the participants. It was also clear that this was conduct to which the men she was working with were not vulnerable, but that Mrs Jones was, even if other female colleagues were not. The Industrial Tribunal found that the behaviour was that to which she as a woman was vulnerable in a way that a man could never have been and thus the incidents fell within the scope of sexual harassment.

Case Four: McKenzie v A Corner Shop

Ms McKenzie worked as a shop assistant. She claimed that the shop owner's behaviour in making verbal and physical sexual advances, including pinning her against a door and licking her face, amounted to sexual harassment. She left as a result. The shop owner denied the allegations. His two male employees called as witnesses denied seeing or being aware of any such behaviour. The Industrial Tribunal in Glasgow thought that it was 'significant' that none of the employer's female employees gave evidence. The Industrial Tribunal preferred the evidence of Ms McKenzie, and found that she had suffered sex discrimination. She was awarded £1,000 for injury to feelings. The Industrial Tribunal said it was 'particularly unpleasant and acutely distressing for a girl of eighteen who was clearly in a vulnerable position'.

Case Five: MacGregor v A Supermarket

Ms MacGregor claimed that she was sexually harassed by her store manager. She claimed sex discrimination on the ground of sexual harassment, and on the ground

that her complaint was not properly handled. The harasser had made crude suggestive remarks, suggestions and gestures when they were alone. The Industrial Tribunal in Inverness found that the employers were liable for the actions of their supervisor. They had no equal opportunities policy, and no supervision or training in sex discrimination. They had reprimanded the supervisor, but left him to apologise and suggested to her that she should move to a different store if she was unable to work with him. She was awarded £3,500 for injury to feelings for 'significant humiliation and distress' by an immediate supervisor twenty years her senior.

Case Six: Anderson v A Discotheque, A Disc Jockey and An Employment Agency

Miss Anderson was a bar-person in a discotheque who claimed sex discrimination against her employers, a self-employed disc-jockey who was

contracted to work for her employers and agents of her employers who had contracted the disc-jockey to work for them. She claimed that the disc-jockey had sexually harassed her by continual verbal comments and physical sexual advances of a vulgar nature which forced her to leave.

The Industrial Tribunal in Glasgow found that although the disc-jockey was self-employed, Miss Anderson's employers were liable under the Sex Discrimination Act for his behaviour. It found that the agents who had contracted the disc-jockey were not liable. She was awarded £4,000 for significant injury to feelings for the upset to her which had lasting effect, in that she became withdrawn and left her job.

• The above is an extract from *Sexual Harassment – how to deal with it*, a briefing produced by the Equal Opportunities Commission. See page 39 for address details.

Men now victims of workplace inequality

By Toby Moore, Industry Editor

Protection for the rights of men in the workplace is likely to dominate the agenda of the Equal Opportunities Commission over the coming years, its chairman said yesterday.

Kamlesh Bahl said the image of men as sole earners in the nuclear family was a 'stereotype which must be addressed' by employers to reflect changing work patterns.

The commission, which this year celebrates its 20th anniversary, has traditionally viewed men as the stimulus to discrimination rather than its victims.

Speaking at a conference on the Economics of Equal Opportunities, in London, Mrs Bahl argued that two factors were now squeezing male employment: the growth in part-time working, which favoured women, and evidence that girls were leaving education better qualified than boys.

'The role of men is continuing

to change,' she said. 'We need to put something in that vacuum.'

Mrs Bahl said that men were also discriminated against in work as changing family roles put pressure on their traditional status as main earner. 'We need to make it quite legitimate that a man, as well as a woman, can go to an employer and say "My child is sick and I need to be home", and not feel guilt,' said Mrs Bahl.

She said that the commission, however, remained concerned by the weight of tradition in the workplace that still meant female managers earned 25 per cent less than their male counterparts.

'The sort of thing we still have to deal with is, for example, that

only 20 per cent of people entering nursing are men, yet 80 per cent of health service managers are male,' said Mrs Bahl.

The conference intended to demonstrate that firms that introduce flexible working, child care arrangements, career breaks and other equality policies gain an economic advantage.

Howard Davies, deputy governor of the Bank of England, said he was 'afflicted by doubts' and that these had sent him to consult economists at the Bank of England. Their response was that discrimination was a desirable activity, but only 'in the sense of seeking to identify the skills and characteristics of the workforce'. He said that discrimination on grounds other than ability and productivity made no sense.

Whatever happened to Pa?

Maureen Freely argues that equality demands that fathers and mothers share the responsibility of rearing their children

Why are men the second sex when it comes to parenthood? Midwives, health visitors, and other family support services reinforce the message that a father's place is not at home. Those who *are* at home, either as house husbands or as babysitters while their wives work part-time, only rarely find a welcome in the informal networks of friends and neighbours that women take for granted.

Even where fathers manage to muddle through, they do so to a large extent without legal safeguards. Although a third of children in Britain are born out of wedlock, and three quarters of these to parents who are living together, unmarried fathers have few rights. The same can be said of divorced fathers whose ex-wives have care of their children. The only way fathers can be reasonably sure of playing a steady and active part in the rearing of their children is by staying married.

These are the conditions under which men in Britain enter and experience fatherhood. An extraordinary number of people seem to think this is as it should be. Men are just not up to the job of looking after children, they say – seldom pausing to question the laws and attitudes that reinforce their prejudices.

Next week the Institute for Public Policy Research is running a conference designed to change all this. In the report due to be published on the same day, they show how – media myths notwithstanding – fathers are playing an ever greater role in the rearing of their children. It is therefore unfair that they should be treated like second-class carers. They deserve statutory paternity leave, training for parenthood, more day to day support, social and medical services that recognise their contribution, and laws that help them stay involved with their children outside marriage and after divorce.

If you believe in equal opportunities for men and women then these proposals are simply common sense. The case for fathers playing more of a role in parenting is being put strongly by women. One of the authors of the report is a woman. So are quite a number of the speakers, so is the chairman of the IPPR. So are most of the people arguing about it in the press. How did fathers' rights become a woman's issue?

And why are feelings riding so high? It has prompted a frantic exchange of articles in this newspaper and elsewhere, followed by a vast number of heated letters from men who are tired of feminist condescension, women who are tired of lazy fathers, women who are equally tired of anti-paternal feminists, and men who think single mothers can be admirable without proving fathers superfluous.

The IPPR report makes reference, almost in passing, about the way in which women's rights depend on fathers' rights. It states that 82 per cent of fathers in Britain work full time, with a third working more than 60 hours a week.

It is logical that if fathers provide the main source of income for their families, they are not likely to risk career breaks, job-shares or part-time work – even if they do want to spend more time with their children than their own fathers spent with them. No matter how good or bad their personal track records, fathers need to be relieved of the work load. The only way forward is to create family-friendly policies that are designed for men as well as women.

In some enlightened workplaces, this is already happening, but they are few and far between. Parental leave is soon to be a statutory right everywhere in the EU except Britain. It already exists in the Nordic countries: in Sweden, 40 per cent of fathers now make use of it. The history of family-friendly policies in countries like Sweden shows how paternal rights go hand in hand with maternal rights.

Where parental leave has been mostly or exclusively for women, it has had the effect of widening the gap between men and women in the workplace. The same policy that gave women time off to spend with their families, has also prevented women from performing as well or being treated equally at work.

It's only when men and women can adjust their work schedules to include time for their families, that women, as a group, can begin to look forward to equal opportunities at work. To put it baldly: women with children are never going to find equal rights with men outside the home unless men have equal rights with women inside it.

Adrienne Burgess, co-author of the conference report, believes that the only way anyone can become a competent parent is by being left in sole charge. 'We learn on the job, and the job is not just a chore but a privilege. There's this fundamental belief that women must seduce men into looking after children, that it's not something they want to do. But the more they do, the more they wrestle with it, the more hugs they get. When my partner takes our child out so that I can work, I no longer think, this is sweet of him. I think, this is his chance!'

Giving a father a chance means giving up the idea that mothers are competent by nature. Many of us did a long time ago – there is a long and honourable tradition of feminists opposing the idea of a maternal instinct and supporting equal parenting. I am not advocating going back to a time where every good house is under a petty patriarch's thumb. Nor do I mean to imply that there is only one right way of bringing up children. I just can't find any justification for good-enough fathers to be not-as good-as-mothers in the eyes of the law.

Any woman wanting the sexes to share power equally is honour bound to consider fathers' as well as mothers' rights. My main motive in writing this is what my own father used to call 'enlightened self-interest': we won't get what we want until they get what they deserve.

© *The Guardian*
April, 1996

Stereotyping and prejudices

Information from the Department for Education and Employment

In the home there are indications that attitudes towards traditional roles are slowly changing. Latest published research shows increasing numbers of people think that household tasks should be shared. In practice however men are still much less likely to undertake tasks such as household cleaning and washing although the proportion that do so is gradually increasing.

In two parent households, childcare remains predominantly the woman's responsibility. The majority of lone parent households are headed by women, and children in their care tend to be younger than children in the care of lone fathers. While the proportion of single mothers has shown a significant increase in the last decade, marital breakdown is the most common reason for the formation of lone parent families. Children who live with only one of their natural parents are more likely to live with their mother: in 1991, 19% of all dependent children lived with their natural mother but not their natural father, while only 3% lived with their natural father but not their natural mother. These children were very likely to be in a lone parent family if they lived with their mother, but those with their natural father were almost as likely to live as step children in a family headed by a couple.

Men's attitudes are particularly relevant in helping to break down stereotyping and changing cultural patterns of conduct, particularly in helping support the reconciliation of domestic and working life. The Government encourages employers to consider the benefits of a wide range of flexible working practices, including part-time working, that can help men and women to reconcile work with their domestic responsibilities.

● The above is an extract from the third report of the *UN Convention on the Elimination of all forms of discrimination against women*.

© *Department for Education and Employment*
July, 1995

In the home there are indications that attitudes towards traditional roles are slowly changing

Helping with the housework

Do you help with the housework? If so then you are probably a man. Why? Because men 'help' with housework, while it is generally assumed to be women's responsibility. Even when a household employs a cleaner or home help, it is the woman who usually pays their wages, however small her own income.

By Shelagh Diplock

Attitude studies now show that the majority of men as well as women believe that the work of looking after a home and family should be shared. Yet even among younger people where this attitude is strongest, and even when the woman works full-time, it is she who still does most of the ironing and cooking. Men may share the washing-up but will seldom clean the toilet.

There are of course a few households where men do all the housework and most people, male or female, who live alone, look after themselves and their own homes perfectly adequately without any 'help' at all. Advertisements that portray men as incapable of using a washing machine or iron are insulting to men. Men are assumed to be proficient when it comes to lawn mowers or power drills.

Such images have undermined the work that men do in the home and women may be tempted to reinforce this by claiming a superior ability. Older women in particular may have difficulty sitting down with their feet up while their husbands do the ironing or hoovering – even if both are retired. They may resist his attempts to take a share of the housework even though he may enjoy it.

This summer Fawcett is launching a new campaign for 'Equal Partnership in the Home' to explore ways in which the gap between attitudes and behaviour can be closed. If couples want to share in the home – how can they be helped to turn that desire into practical reality? We will be bringing together men and women facing changes in their lives: moving in together, the birth of a first baby, retirement from employment – to hear their views on the problems and possible solutions.

Conflict in relationships over sharing at home is an increasing problem. Many young couples share housework to a greater or lesser extent when they are both working full-time and there are no children. However when children come along and one partner gives up paid work or moves to a part-time job then this sharing may become more uneven or cease altogether.

Many men still do not understand the work involved in looking after small children. They resent being asked to do household chores when they come home from a long day at work. A woman is assumed to have plenty of time to do all this during the day. It is not surprising, given that a mother's work is normally described as 'housework' not caring or mothering. If a woman is tired at the end of a day then they are 'not managing properly'.

Taking a job, full-time or part-time, may provide a legitimacy for her exhaustion and be seen as an escape route. Resentment and conflict which surround the reality of lack of partnership at home, when both partners have the expectation that sharing is what ought to happen, can undermine relationships and cause unhappiness to both parties. In the long run helping men and women to share at home may be one of the best ways to improve their quality of life.

● The above is an extract from *Towards Equality*, published by the Fawcett Society. See page 39 for address details.

© Fawcett Society
Summer, 1996

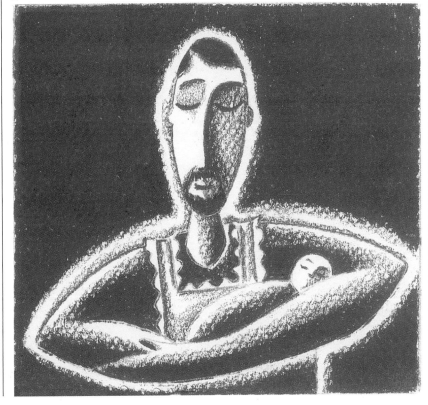

A woman's place is in the wider world

From a vast statistical survey, Maurice Weaver discerns a picture of gradual improvements in the home, the workplace and society

The most detailed survey ever published on the lives of British women appears today, presenting a broad brush study of how they are managing their lives in a fast-changing society – from teenagers to pensioners.

It suggests that most are coping rather well. The picture presented is of healthy and resilient – if sometimes stressed – women whose quality of life at home, in the workplace and in the world is an improvement on that of previous generations.

Full equality in the labour market remains elusive, says the Central Statistical Office's (CSO) publication, *Social Focus on Women*.

But women are better educated, more assertive and traditional woman-man stereotypes of home-maker and breadwinner have been eroded beyond recall.

Even the picture on the report's glossy cover conveys a message of cool and confident wellbeing.

It shows a competent-looking and Hepburnesque working mother balancing a plump baby, leather briefcase, toy duck and dossier while looking quite dazzling in pearls and business jacket. A male ideal it may be, but it does reflect in some measure the relatively up-beat tenor of a report that is edited by two women, Jenny Church and Carol Summerfield.

Their brief was to 'paint a picture of women's lives today' and show 'how they have been changing'. The answer to the latter question seems to be – a lot.

Women are still underrepresented at the top in business, it concedes, and they earn less than men.

But they are increasingly setting marriage aside in their younger years to play a more active role in commerce and the professions. Socially, they are going to pubs, night classes and sports clubs as never before. They exhibit greater self-reliance and are broader-minded (30,000 read *Penthouse*).

The Central Statistical Office's (male) spokesman says one objective of the study is to give 'a different perspective' on other recent reports, notably that from the Equal Opportunities Commission whose *National Agenda for Action* last summer was heavy with references to women's victimhood. The commission complained of employment inequalities.

The CSO, on the other hand, points out that 55 per cent of women work full-time; they are making inroads into the professions and are affected less by long-term unemployment than are men. The commission shed tears about the pressures on working mothers. The CSO talks of more women on the pill and delaying families until they are in their 30s and financially settled. Lone mothers may be a symbol of the times, it says, but more than three-quarters have husbands or partners.

While the commission bequeathed a sense of gender gloom, the CSO report presents a happier image. Women are better off, it says (three-quarters carry credit cards) and better housed (17 per cent are buying their own homes, twice the figure for a decade ago).

In a frivolous sense, the survey offers ammunition for friendly domestic repartee. A wife who quotes the old epithet that a woman's work is never done, might find her attention drawn to page 54 which reveals that British females watch television for an average of 28 hours a week.

A husband's argument about politics might produce a reference to page 51 which shows that less than seven per cent of women show much interest in what is going on at Westminster. The document can also provide ready support for headaches. Stress is increasingly a female complaint, it says.

The CSO has not done all this work merely to satisfy a hankering for trivia. It has an eye on the UN conference on women's issues next month in Beijing.

The message from Britain is that things are looking up.

© *The Telegraph plc London, 1995*

If the job fits

Male and female employment by type of occupation

% of group — Women / Men

Bank Managers, PAs, GPs, School Teachers, Nurses, Police Officers, W'sale Reps, Catering Assistants

Fem and us

So men are up in arms about discrimination at work, are they? Does this mean that the feminists have won the sex war? Maureen Freely thinks not

This, apparently, is the day we've all been waiting for. Not since prehistory have we had it so good. Men are finally losing the sex war! According to figures to be published by the Equal Opportunities Commission next month, 820 men complained about discrimination in job recruitment last year, with only 803 complaints coming from women.

It's when men seek employment as nurses and secretaries that they run into trouble. Their prospective employers pass them over because they are afraid these men might be after their jobs, or might not smile when asked to make a cup of coffee – or worse, might not smile fetchingly. There seems to be a consensus out there that most customers prefer to be greeted by young, pretty women.

The other nice thing about young, pretty women – and the older, plainer matrons they inevitably become – is that they accept lower pay and part-time hours. The reason they are willing to do this, people say, is that they are just in it for pin money; they have their families to think about and their breadwinning husbands to depend on.

But the economy has changed now – even the *Daily Mail* admits it. Yesterday, it quoted NatWest's chief economist as saying that within the next five years, the number of full-time jobs in this country will shrink, but that opportunities for part-timers will rise by one and a half million. Most of these new jobs will go to presentable, amenable women who can make coffee with a smile.

They will probably be smiling because they're so glad to get out of the house, because more and more of these houses will contain husbands who have been made redundant and cannot find real jobs – or even, if the new EOC figures are anything to go by, joke pin money work. No household can run on pin money, but pin money is better than no money at all. Next time you go to Sainsbury's at an unsocial hour and see a woman with huge rings under her eyes check out your groceries, don't make the mistake of pitying her. This woman's present is your future.

She represents what Piers Paul Read writing in the *Daily Mail* calls 'the latest nail in the coffin of masculine status'. If she liked things the way they used to be, then the victory of feminism – which the EOC figures are supposed to represent – becomes all the more amazing.

Business has less and less interest in men with muscles who know how to bargain collectively

Just think about it: 25 years ago, there was hardly a kitchen without a woman in an apron and hardly a desk that didn't come with a man in a dark suit. Now there are more suits than desks and millions of women working part-time – this despite the fact that, according to current popular opinion, most men, women and children long to turn back the clock. How did these feminists manage to push through their programme when there was so little support? And what diabolical ploys did they use against the press, which has been tireless in its efforts to advertise the dangers of the feminist threat?

Hardly a day goes by when it doesn't hit the headlines, powered by women known, generically, as 'the feminists'. They always act as one and they haven't changed their mind about anything since 1973. Which is why, if a woman wins a marital rape or sexual harassment case, no matter what its merits, we'll hear that 'the feminists' are happy about it. If the man she has accused wins instead the same papers will tell us 'the feminists' are up in arms.

This is the other strange thing about the endless string of feminist victories against masculinity and family values. Most women suing for sexual harassment or going to the EOC to complain about job discrimination do not call themselves feminists. Like the men who complain to the EOC, they just want a decent life. If I went around the offices of the EOC itself, I'm sure I would hear the same things I hear everywhere else: that men are not the enemy and that feminism as it has been characterised in the popular press has no relevance to the nineties. Despite all this, the media still carries on its desperate love affair with the battle of the sexes, talking of wars and victories, reversals, causes, campaigns and feminist Machiavellis.

One of these days, a great prophet is going to look down from a mountain top and see that we are not in the midst of a sex war but just another economic revolution. Business has less and less interest in men with muscles who know how to bargain collectively. It has a lot to gain from docile female employees who cannot afford to talk back – or work full-time, or even leave home. This prophet is going to understand that while this is bad news for men, it is not very good news for women either, or for anyone trying to use part-time workers' joke wages to support a family. But the people for whom it will be the worst news of all will be the captains of industry, or whatever they'll be calling themselves in the 21st century. How will the public respond to the news that *they* are the feminists who fought and won all those victories?

© *The Guardian*
April, 1996

The future challenges

Information from the Equal Opportunities Commission

There have been major gains for sex equality over the last twenty years but the EOC faces a very different society and world of work in the mid-1990s than when it was established in the mid-1970s.

The rate of economic growth, the shifts in world markets and the future of the European Union, particularly its future direction on economic regeneration and social policy more broadly, have major implications for progress on sex equality.

At the same time, the ever-changing world of work – with its shifts from manufacturing to services; from permanent and full-time work to part-time, temporary and casual work; from employment creation in large firms to the growth in small/medium ones; from regulated to de-regulated labour markets and from skilled manual jobs to white collar knowledge-based jobs – will create both challenges and opportunities for us.

Overlaid on these factors and trends are the changes in house-hold, family and society which have a significant influence on the labour market, participation of individual men and women and on the demands on the social security systems.

The EOC's experience shows that there is a lifecycle of discrimination that starts from the choices made at an early age. These are compounded by inequalities in access to education and training, occupational segregation, unequal pay, inequitable sharing of caring responsibilities culminating for many women in dependency on the State especially in old age. This lifecycle is demonstrated for the first time in the EOC's publication *Women and Men in Britain* launched on 20 July 1995.

Milestones for progress

It is clear that continued progress on sex equality requires action to challenge discrimination at each stage of the lifecycle. The EOC has identified a number of goals which, when achieved, will serve as milestones on the path to equality. These are set out below:

- simplified and accessible laws and procedures for those who complain of discrimination
- an effective mechanism in place to evaluate policy options and proposed legislation for disproportionate impact on one sex
- an improved system of maternity rights and a national strategy in place to provide good quality, affordable childcare available to all
- an education and training system in which significant inequalities in access and opportunity have been eliminated
- a significant increase in the numbers of women in decision-making, particularly where they have traditionally been under-represented
- equal status for part-time workers in statute enshrined in job contracts and in practice
- official statistics collected in a form which allows analysis by gender, ethnicity and, where appropriate, type of employment
- a substantial decrease in the number of jobs segregated on the basis of sex
- increases in the numbers of men sharing caring responsibilities and in the value society places on this work
- an expansion in statutory and contractual paternity, parental and family leave provision
- a substantial narrowing of the earnings gap between women and men
- structural changes to the state pension system to increase the numbers of women able to achieve a full entitlement in their own right
- reform of the social security system to meet more closely the future patterns of men and women's working lives.

The above is an extract from *Sex discrimination does not pay*, a publication produced by the Equal Opportunities Commission.

© *Equal Opportunities Commission*

Fair Play . . .

Regional partnerships for equality

What is Fair Play?

Fair Play is the first joint Government/EOC partnership, and was established to tackle the barriers facing women in economic and social life. It was launched on 25 April 1994 by David Hunt, then Secretary of State for Employment, and Kamlesh Bahl, Chairwoman of the EOC.

Fair Play aims to help women realise their full capabilities so they can make their full contribution to the local economy and the local community. Fair Play is about:
● competitiveness
● equality of opportunity
● partnership.

Why do we need Fair Play?

There are very strong economic and business reasons. Over half the population and nearly half the workforce is female. The proportion of women in the workforce has been increasing and this trend is likely to continue. So it is vital to access and retain the talents of women in the workforce, in public life and in the voluntary sector. Anything less than Fair Play deprives the country of the full contribution of all its people.

Who is supporting Fair Play?

At both national and regional levels, Fair Play has the support of a wide range of key organisations representing the public, private and voluntary sectors as well as from women's groups.

How does it work?

Through consortia of local people established in each English region. Each consortium decides its own structure, composition and agenda.

What is a consortium?

A consortium is an association or group of organisations who come

EQUAL OPPORTUNITIES COMMISSION

together to work in partnership towards an agreed strategy and specific objectives. The structure of the Fair Play consortium varies from region to region.

Are consortia tackling the same issues in every region?

No. Consortia can't tackle everything, so they are setting clear and measurable goals linked to agreed local priorities for action. They are also being encouraged to exchange ideas and avoid duplication of effort.

Many other groups are tackling the barriers facing women – why did we need another initiative?

Fair Play is not just another initiative, but a unique model of working together and getting things done by:
● identifying key local players
● promoting a partnership approach
● bringing together current activity
● identifying areas of overlap and gaps
● developing a shared agenda which offers economies of scale
● implementing a regional agenda for action.

What are the benefits of this partnership approach?

The benefits are considerable:
● pooling of knowledge, experience, expertise and good practice

● more efficient use of resources and economies of scale
● raising the profile of issues and challenges
● the ability to attract funding from other agencies.

Where is the money coming from?

The Government is providing pump priming funds for the first three years to help the consortia to develop and begin to implement their action plans. Further funding is coming from:
● sponsorship from local and national organisations
● a number of European, national and regional budgets.

How can my organisation get involved?

Different arrangements apply around the country. There may be opportunities to be involved:
● as a member of the regional consortium or of a task force or ad-hoc working group
● by offering professional or specialist expertise
● by sponsoring consortia activity in cash or kind, including full- or part-time secondments
● by passing on relevant information about local research and effective practice to the consortia for them to disseminate throughout the region.

How do I find out more?

Contact either the Fair Play Regional Co-ordinator for your region or the Department for Education and Employment / Equal Opportunities Commission National Co-ordinators.

In pursuit of equality

A national agenda for action

No country can claim to have achieved human rights for all its citizens until the human rights of all women, regardless of age, marital status, ethnic background or disability are in practice equal, integral and inalienable.

This National Agenda for Action has been drawn up by the Women's National Commission and the Equal Opportunities Commissions for Great Britain and Northern Ireland, in consultation with, and endorsed by, organisations representing millions of women throughout the UK. It provides a basis for UK implementation of the Global Platform for Action agreed at the United Nations Fourth World Conference on Women. The Platform constitutes a plan of action to improve women's lives and to achieve equal treatment for women and men. But commitment to it by governments will be meaningless unless specific action is taken to implement it nationally.

This Agenda highlights the essential issues that must be addressed by government and by decision makers in other organisations including local government, political parties, business and the voluntary sector to achieve equality.

Political issues

- All proposed new legislation and, periodically, existing legislation to be evaluated for its impact on equality between the sexes.
- Additional measures to improve women's participation in decision-making, particularly where they have traditionally been underrepresented, e.g. in elected positions, in senior positions in the public and private sectors, and in the media.

- Simplified, accessible laws and procedures for the prevention and redress of discrimination.
- Equal treatment for women in all areas of nationality, citizenship and immigration.

Social issues

- Equal rights and protection for all workers irrespective of their patterns of work or status.
- A national strategy to provide good quality, affordable childcare available to all.
- A simplified and comprehensive system of maternity rights and protection, which recognises the fundamental importance of maternal and infant well-being.
- Action to encourage and facilitate a culture of shared responsibility between men and women, including the introduction of statutory paternity, parental and family leave and the encouragement of family-friendly work practices.
- Measures to ensure that the publicly funded education and training system provides equality of opportunity for both sexes and promotes equality between men

and women throughout their lifetime. Employers to be encouraged to provide training and retraining of girls and women equally with boys and men.
- Recognition of the full value of the social and economic contribution of those who care for dependents of whatever age.
- Provision of the necessary support to meet their needs.
- Equality of access by women and men to the mass media.
- Action to end the exploitation of women's sexuality by the media, the stereotyping of their portrayal and the trivialisation of their interests.
- Strong, preventive measures and sanctions against violence against women. Legislative and practical support for victims of violence.

Health

- Full recognition of the different physical and mental health care needs of women and men, and equality in treatment and in access to health care provision.

Economic issues

- Initiatives to tackle poverty which disproportionately affects women, e.g. by reform of the tax, benefits and pensions systems, focusing on measures to ensure the economic independence of the individual throughout life.
- Action to close the gap between women's and men's earnings through measures such as simplified and effective equal pay legislation.
- Encouragement of men and women to enter non-traditional areas of work and work patterns.
- Equalisation of access to welfare benefits for men and women, including the introduction of widowers' benefits.

Monitoring

- Publication of all official statistics by gender and, where possible, ethnicity, age and disability, in order to measure progress and to identity areas for future action.

In this Agenda we set out the key principles on which action to improve women's lives in the UK should be based. A series of working documents analysing the issues and proposing specific, detailed action under each item will supplement it, based on work by, and consultation with, women's organisations as well as the WNC and the EOCs.

The Equal Opportunities Commissions and the Women's National Commission are calling on the Government, political party leaders, business and the voluntary sector, and others to commit themselves to taking action to implement this Agenda.

We also seek to raise awareness of the issues as widely as possible, and invite individual women and men to lend their support.

What you as an individual can do to support this Agenda

- Talk to others about the issues.
- Ask for further copies of this leaflet and circulate them to people who might be interested, or are in a position to achieve change.
- Raise the Agenda in any group or organisation you belong to. Ask them to register support.
- Ask your MP what he or she will do to see that the Agenda is implemented.
- Write to your local or national newspapers about the Agenda.

You can make your voice heard as a citizen, as a voter, or through organisations you belong to, to ensure that the commitments made at the World Conference on Women are not forgotten and lead to action, not just words.

The Women's National Commission is the official, independent advisory body responsible for ensuring that women's views are heard by the Government. Its members are major women's organisations, representing women of all backgrounds, ages and walks of life, a variety of interests and a range of opinion across the political spectrum.

The Equal Opportunities Commission for Great Britain was established by the Sex Discrimination Act 1975. The EOC for Northern Ireland was established by the Sex Discrimination (Northern Ireland) Order 1976. The legislation in both cases had all party support. The Commissions are the independent, statutory bodies working to eliminate discrimination and to promote equality between women and men. Commissioners are drawn from both the public and private sectors, including from business and commerce, trade unions, the voluntary sector, education and professional bodies.

© *Central Office of Information for the Women's National Commission*

Women's participation in the labour market

Although a smaller proportion of women than men participate in the UK labour market, their activity rates are getting closer to those of men so that women now account for 44% of the labour force. From 1984 to 1994 the economic activity rate in Great Britain for women of working age rose from 66% to 70%, while that for men has more recently fallen from 88% to 85%. The economic activity rate for women aged 25 to 34 years rose by over 25 percentage points between 1971 and 1993, a greater increase then for any other groups. This increase may be partly attributable to an increase in the average age at which women have children. Women aged from 45-70 are significantly less likely to be economically active though their participation is likely to increase in future: for example, in 1993, 54.6% of women aged 55-59 years were working compared to 75.4% of men.

Economic activity rates vary between ethnic groups. In spring 1994, 75% of White women aged between 25 and 44 were economically active compared with 71% from the Black ethnic group, much smaller than the gap between men of the same age from these two ethnic groups. However, just under one in four Pakistani and Bangladeshi women were economically active.

With regard to women with health problems or disabilities expected to last more than a year, Labour Force Survey estimates indicate that 36% of women with health problems are economically active (in employment or ILO unemployed) compared with 75% for those without health problems – compared to 47% and 84% of men for the same categories. ILO unemployment is higher for women with health problems: 18% compared with 7% for women without health problems, a similar disparity to that of men.

Mothers' participation has also increased, the only exception to the trend being lone parents, whatever their qualification levels. The age of the youngest dependent child is a more significant factor affecting the activity rates of mothers than the number of dependent children.

Unique among EU member states, the UK has a lower unemployment rate for women than men for all age groups. In addition, the UK unemployment rate for women is below the EU average. In spring 1994, ILO unemployment rates were 24% for Pakistani/Bangladeshi women, though all these rates are lower than the comparative figures for men.

- The above is an extract from the *UN Convention on the elimination of all forms of discrimination against women.*

© *Department for Education and Employment*

The post-equality generation

Facts about young women in the 1990s

It is 25 years since the Equal Pay Act was passed and 20 years since the Sex Discrimination Act became law. These events may not so far have brought real economic and social equality for women, but they have had a profound effect on the values and aspirations of the generation which has grown up in their wake.

There are 7.5 million young women between 18-34 in the UK today, around one sixth of the voting population. This 'post-equality cohort' is the first to have benefited entirely from the battles of the women's rights movements of the seventies. They not only expect equal rights, but the freedom to progress in their careers and to share caring responsibilities.

Along with the disappearance of traditional male roles in the workforce, this change in women's attitudes to work, family and authority has had a profound effect on British values overall. In contrast to those over 55, today's young people are not committed to the distinct gender roles which led women to accept the restrictions of the past.

More women are working than ever before. They want to work, to be economically independent, to choose when and whether to have a family, and expect to be able to continue their careers. They are ambitious and, when they find their expectations aren't fulfilled or if the burden of care still isn't being shared, they are increasingly frustrated.

Education

Young women in the 1990s are the most highly educated of any generation. Over 90% of 16-34 year old women have some level of academic qualification, and they are coming out of the education system more ambitious and with better results than boys, outnumbering and outperforming them at every stage, from GCSE to degree level. However, the gender division in choice of subject matter at A-level is still apparent, with young women favouring languages, art and literature, while young men choose science and maths. For those who take up youth training the choices are also different, with more young women studying business administration, and men subjects such as engineering and building.

Work

Whatever the subject, young women's educational achievement brings higher expectations and a greater desire to be successful in the workplace. Unlike older generations, very few young women believe they should stay at home while the man works. In fact, female workforce participation rates have risen while male participation has fallen, and work is now a primary factor in most women's lives.

Research by DEMOS shows a profound shift in women's attitude to success across the social spectrum. Four out of five young women want to work or develop a career. Even those who work just to earn a living are strongly attached to the idea of employment as a means of identity.

Women in their twenties and thirties without childcare commitments now have broadly similar employment patterns to men and the gender pay gap overall is small (although regional differences can be greater). But problems still occur when women have to combine the responsibilities of family and employment.

Family and the 'care deficit'

Women are having children much later. Ten years ago women usually

Few young women believe they should stay at home while the man works

had their first child in their early twenties. Now it's more common to wait until the late twenties, even early thirties, so a working pattern can be established first.

But young women's career aspirations typically become frustrated when they become parents. There is a huge gap between their expectations, needs and the infrastructure to support them. Although male attitudes to working mothers have changed, young women still shoulder the burden of domestic responsibilities – while their earnings are making up a vital and growing part of household income. This 'care deficit' is one of the major pressures on women today and can still destroy career progress.

Part-time work is often the only option for many women who want and need to continue working. But research shows that most return to work at a lower level and with a lower income than before. It is at this stage in their lives that overall, young women's hourly earnings start to drop relative to men's. And their ambitions are frustrated – one in three working mothers feel they have skills which are not being applied.

But young women are determined to try and maintain their progress. They are less likely to fit work around school hours than before, using formal childcare arrangements such as nurseries or childminders. But they carry the burden financially, as two thirds of working mothers under 35 pay the cost of the childcare themselves. The majority would like their employers to support them in offering childcare facilities, but few do. And so there is a serious shortfall in the provision of public sector care.

This 'care crisis' is having a huge impact on an able and ambitious generation of young women. It creates great stress, limits their choice of work, the progress in their careers, their financial security, and their ability to take part in public life on an equal basis.

New professions

In professional life, young women have made the greatest advances of any other generation. Women now account for 38% of professional jobs

and, overall, the pay gap is least in this sector. There are now more female solicitors under 30 than male. Over a third of the new chartered accountants are female. The proportion of women who are corporate managers and administrators doubled during the eighties.

Young women's career aspirations typically become frustrated when they become parents

------

But at a managerial level, the pressure on women to prove themselves is intense, and young female managers work the longest hours of anyone in the UK. Women managers believe their work is less highly valued than men's. There is frustration at the 'glass ceiling' preventing women from progressing and even those who have broken

through are paid, on average, 16% less than their male counterparts.

On the margins

Despite the huge progress made by women over the last 20 years, there is a significant proportion of young women who have not benefited from the post-equality era. For those without qualifications or skills, employment has not increased and the pay gap remains significant. If partners are unemployed, there is often a disincentive for them to work. Lower paid workers have less access to formal childcare and depend much more on their partner and working part-time. Young low-income workers have the highest level of frustrated ambition.

But those most disconnected from women's economic and social progress are single parents. There are 1.4m lone parents in the UK, the highest proportion among 25-34 year old women. They are more likely to live in poverty than any other family, and they too are often better off financially if they don't work.

© *Fawcett Society Newsletter, 1996*

Division of household tasks

Who does what?

All respondents were asked how tasks should be shared. Those who were married or cohabiting were asked how tasks were actually shared. Only married and cohabiting couples with children under 18 living in the same household were asked about child rearing.

	Actual allocation of tasks %			How tasks should be shared %		
	Mainly woman	Mainly man	Shared equally	Mainly woman	Mainly man	Shared equally
Household shopping	45	8	47	82	1	16
Making evening meal	70	9	20	39	1	57
Doing evening dishes	33	28	37	11	1	75
Doing household cleaning	68	4	27	36	1	62
Doing washing and ironing	84	3	12	58	0	40
Repairing household equipment	6	82	10	1	66	31
Organising household money and bills	40	31	28	14	17	66
Looking after sick children	60	1	39	37	0	60
Teaching children discipline	17	9	73	4	8	85

Source: MORI, Whirlpool Foundation

Expectations for the future

An investigation into the self-esteem of 13 and 14 year old girls and boys

What's happening to today's 13 and 14 year olds?

Increasingly, girls are doing better than boys at school.[1] Does this mean that we can stop worrying about equal opportunities for women at work because everything will sort itself out when today's young teenagers enter the workforce? What do girls and boys worry about and what makes them feel good about themselves? What do we, as adults, need to do in order to help both boys and girls achieve their potential in later life?

For the first time in the UK we can start to understand these questions from the perspective of the boys and girls whose current views, hopes and fears will create the basis of our society in the 21st century. New research commissioned by the Health Education Authority in April 1995 provides a unique insight into the world of young people in Britain today, and raises intriguing questions about the different ways in which boys and girls acquire self-confidence and approach their futures.

Key findings

- Children get most enjoyment from spending time with their friends and spending money.

- They worry a lot about exams, future jobs and careers.

- Girls worry more than boys, have less self-confidence and are very concerned about their appearance and being liked and admired by others.

- Boys expect to be competitive, take risks and have little difficulty in standing out from the crowd.

- Girls of 13 and 14 are trying to grow up as fast as possible while boys are happy to remain children.

- Parents are an important source of self-esteem for children; teachers are not.

- Both boys and girls find it hard to see a connection between doing well at school and their future jobs and careers.

- Girls expect to have to choose between work and motherhood. They do not want to appear conspicuous or challenge the status quo.

- Boys believe they will be responsible for their family, and expect to be successful in the workplace.

[1] Department for Education figures show that 46.4% of girls are achieving five or more grades A–C at GCSE compared with 37.0% of boys. In 1992, 61.8% of girls and 45.9% of boys gained grades A–C in English, while 73.7% of girls and 69.2% of boys achieved these grades in Physics.

- The above is an extract from *Expectations for the future – An investigation into the self-esteem of 13 and 14 year old girls and boys,* published by the Health Education Authority.

© *Health Education Authority 1996*

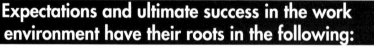

Expectations and ultimate success in the work environment have their roots in the following:

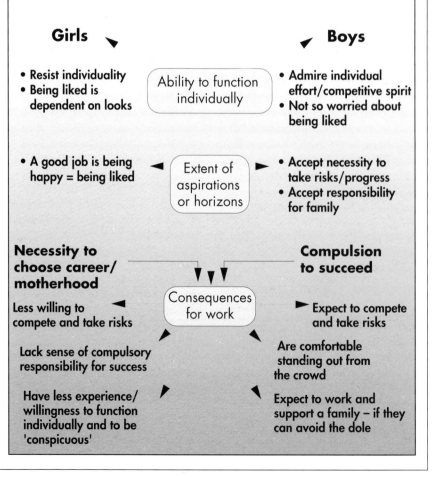

Girls

- Resist individuality
- Being liked is dependent on looks

Ability to function individually

Boys

- Admire individual effort/competitive spirit
- Not so worried about being liked

- A good job is being happy = being liked

Extent of aspirations or horizons

- Accept necessity to take risks/progress
- Accept responsibility for family

Necessity to choose career/motherhood

Compulsion to succeed

Consequences for work

Less willing to compete and take risks

Expect to compete and take risks

Lack sense of compulsory responsibility for success

Are comfortable standing out from the crowd

Have less experience/ willingness to function individually and to be 'conspicuous'

Expect to work and support a family – if they can avoid the dole

Boys' and girls' views of each other

Both boys and girls are quite perceptive about each others' concerns. Boys are particularly convinced that girls are obsessed with their clothes and personal appearance. Interestingly, they perceive this as being part of the girls' effort to gain their approval, to 'get a man', and do not fully appreciate how important appearance is to girls' fundamental sense of self-esteem.

Across all social classes, boys see girls as generally self-absorbed and less concerned with what is happening in the outside world, such as in politics or the environment. Their loyalty to their peer group, in boys' eyes, means that girls are indiscreet and can't be trusted to keep a secret. They believe that girls overwhelmingly worry about the opinion of others, doing the 'right' thing and avoiding embarrassment. In the classroom, girls are seen as being less confident and less likely to get their views across. In the public world boys feel that girls abdicate responsibility to them – 'they can't even order a drink themselves' – making boys feel 'put upon'.

However, there are major discrepancies between the way children of one sex see themselves and how they are perceived by their peers of the opposite sex. Boys perceive girls to be far more able than girls believe themselves to be, in terms of passing exams, going on to further education and having a successful career. For example, while only 6% of girls feel very confident about passing exams, 25% of boys believe girls to be very confident in this respect.

Girls tend to have a rather low opinion of their male peers, believing them to be less thoughtful with a 'couldn't care less' attitude. They suspect, however, that boys really do have similar concerns to their own, but that they are better at masking this by superficial self-assurance, or hiding behind 'silly' behaviour, thus avoiding facing up to problems or losing face with their friends. Girls rate boys noticeably lower on their confidence about educational and career development than do the boys themselves. Personal concerns are largely private matters for boys, in contrast to the girls' frequent

> **Across all social classes, boys see girls as generally self absorbed and less concerned with what is happening in the outside world**

expression of their concerns within their peer group. Girls express a hint of envy that boys are able to appear more confident and at ease with themselves. They themselves experience difficulty in knowing how to 'be themselves', particularly in public arenas. At the same time, girls suspect that the boys' bravado only confirms their relative immaturity and inability to cope with difficult situations. Their suspicion that boys may not be as confident as they appear is to an extent confirmed by the fact that only 25% of boys (compared to 18% of girls) feel very confident about answering questions in class.

● The above is an extract from *Expectations for the future – An investigation into the self-esteem of 13 and 14 year old girls and boys*, published by the Health Education Authority.

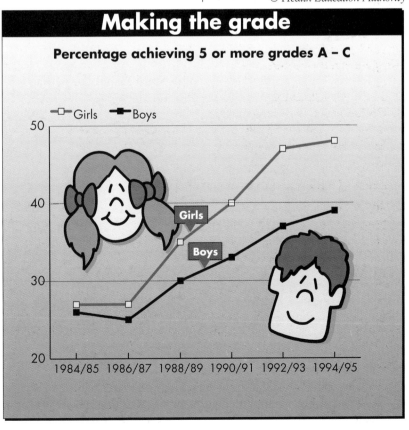

Making the grade

Percentage achieving 5 or more grades A – C

Girls get violent

Girls are beating boys in exams. Young women have moved into former male preserves like the professions. Feminism has brought greater equality. But is it also leading more women to resort to physical violence? Rebecca Fowler reports

There is something uniquely shocking in the image of young women using physical violence against their own sex. We have come to expect violence from boys. We had better get used to more of it from girls.

Scant details have emerged of the events that led up to Louise Allen, 13, lifeless, being rushed to hospital, reportedly after she was set upon by a group of girls 'like a pack of animals' after she left a funfair close to her home in Corby, Northamptonshire, on Monday evening. Even in a violent age the news of her death was met with disbelief.

For the community who knew Louise her death is being treated as a terrible and isolated tragedy that has shaken the Roman Catholic school where she was a popular pupil. But it is bound to fuel concern over the increasing evidence that young girls are more violent, often to one another, than women of older generations. Of course, it is a myth that girls are little angels. Traditionally, they controlled their patch of the playground with manipulation and verbal abuse, including spreading rumours and excluding members of a group. But, until recently, they had not resorted widely to physical violence.

The rise in violent female crime and the increase in reports of female bullying suggest that girls are using violence with almost as much enthusiasm as boys. Women's lives have been transformed by a growing sense of equality with men, yet it is as if the next generation of women are taking up some of the darkest aspects of male behaviour and making it part of their own response to their frustrations and fears.

In the past five years female violent crime has risen by 12 per cent, four times the rate among men, and offences involving women carrying out assault, robbery, murder and drug-related crimes has increased by 250 per cent since 1973. Although the numbers remain small, with 9,500 women found guilty of violence against another person in 1994 compared to 5,300 in 1984, a clear pattern is emerging: women are becoming more violent.

The steady increase in violent crimes among women, especially those in their teens, is forcing a reassessment of the relationship between women, violence and power

---

Most disturbing are the signs of increased violence among younger women who, at the most extreme level, are forming menacing American-style gangs on some inner-city housing estates. (Elizabeth Hurley, the actress and model, was famously mugged by such a gang in London last year.) In a survey by Demos, the independent think-tank, it emerges that in the 15 to 17 age group, girls are more likely to take pleasure in violence than boys, suggesting that we may have a new generation of female aggressors in the making.

Among the most disturbing recent cases were two 17-year-old girls who carried out a vicious attack in 1992 on their 70-year-old neighbour, in which they strangled her with a dog chain; two women who tortured and burned a 16-year-old girl to death in Manchester; and a host of recent crimes in America, from where the trend of female gangs has already started to catch on.

Kidscape, a child protection charity, has seen an increase in the number of calls from girls who are the victims of violent attacks by other girls. The charity received 80 reports of violence in 1993, which rose to 97 in 1994 and to 119 in 1995, varying from kicking and pushing to one group attack in which a girl was pinned down in the showers by classmates who pushed a bar of soap into her anus.

Michel Elliott, director of Kidscape, says young women are getting a confusing message: 'A lot of girls think that to be emancipated one acts like a boy. There is a whole genre of films in which the heroine is

violent,' she says. 'Combined with that, we don't explain the consequences of violence to girls in the same way that we do to boys, because we don't think we need to. They see someone get kicked in a film and get up. They don't understand the consequences.'

The cultural backdrop in which women are portrayed as more assertive, and more aggressive, began to change most notably in the early Nineties. The film *Thelma and Louise*, in which two friends reap a trail of revenge against violent and oppressive men, appealed to an older generation of women who have fought for a hard-won sense of equality. Ms Elliott is among those who believe it conveys ambiguous messages to younger girls: 'There is a tremendous role confusion for girls, but look at the role models we are giving them. We've gone from Doris Day to Drew Barrymore with a gun in *Bad Girls*. This is women trying to be more like men, but instead of taking the best traits, like assertiveness, they've gone for the worst: violence.'

Women have always been portrayed as talented practitioners of evil, but it is as if Lady Macbeth has finally taken up the dagger herself. *Thelma and Louise* was followed by a host of films with subversive violent heroines including *Basic Instinct*, *The Last Seduction* and *Single White Female*. More recently, *Heavenly Creatures* and *Tank Girl* both portrayed younger women who seized their independence through violence.

The 2,000-strong Demos survey of 18 to 34-year-olds made it clear that women had become more assertive. They are just as likely to travel, rock-climb and bungee jump as men. There are now more female solicitors under 30 than male, and gradually women are ascending to the top positions in their professions. Women have also won the basic right to equal opportunities in work and education, something that was unheard of half a century ago.

But for a generation of women who have inherited the fruits of feminism there is a risk of also taking on the most negative aspects of a society once controlled exclusively by men. Heart disease and alcoholism are rising in women, female harassment against men is also on the increase, and the early evidence suggests the connection between violence and poverty is as strong in women as it is in men.

Nick Winkfield, a partner in MORI, the opinion polling organisation, which conducted the research for Demos, says: 'Women in the lower social groups are much more tolerant of violence and more willing to use force to get what they want, compared to well-off women.'

Women who have committed atrocious and notorious crimes, from Myra Hindley to Rosemary West, have been dismissed as so far beyond the pale that it is impossible to draw conclusions from their actions. But the steady increase in violent crimes among women, especially those in their teens, is forcing a reassessment of the relationship between women, violence and power.

Those who work with children believe that the most significant factor in the rise in female crime is the exposure of all young people to violence. Peter Wilson, director of Young Minds, which campaigns for children's mental well-being, explained:

'Women may have become more assertive, but across the genders violence is often the response to a violent upbringing, combined with the fact that children are now exposed to a host of violent images on television.'

Despite the increase in female violence it is significant that girls are still reluctant to be known to be violent. Research at Sheffield University into bullying among 7,000 children suggests that girls are just as likely to use physical violence when they are bullied as boys, but they are ashamed to admit to it. Although women are becoming more violent, there is not yet the equivalent of the macho culture of violence which thrives among boys. That reluctance to boast about violence may offer some hope of containing the rise in female aggression. But the statistics suggest that female violence may well be here to stay – in which case the playground is set to become an even more frightening place than it already is.

© *The Independent*
May, 1996

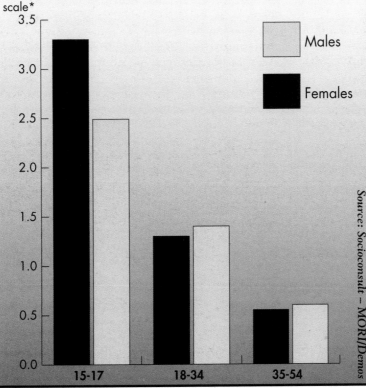

How women are becoming more aggressive

Taking pleasure in violence

* The index was derived from responses to questions asked of 1,511 people in 1994. Questions asked included: "Do you agree that violence can sometimes be exciting?", "Do you agree that it is acceptable to use physical force to get what you want?"

scale*

Males

Females

15-17   18-34   35-54

Source: Sociocomsult – MORI/Demos

The girl child

Status of women: From invisibility to official recognition

The Fourth World Women's Conference was held in Beijing, China in September 1995. ACWW's input into the 'Platform for Action' (designed to address the problems facing women) was underpinned by a staunch belief that practical steps taken by govern-ments will ensure a real and measur-able advance in the situation of women and the girl child worldwide. The 1989 Convention on the Rights of the Child proclaims the right to equality between boys and girls, yet girls still suffer various kinds of deprivation. A vast gap still exists between law and practice. Statistics presented at the International Conference on Population and Development and the World Summit for Social/Development show how the number of children born, as well as their health and well-being, are linked to the mothers' rights and educational level.

The early years

Very early in life, girls usually find themselves taking second place to boys, who grow up with different expectations. The differences can be life-threatening – for example, when a girl in a poor family receives inadequate food or medical care compared with her brother.

Since the Convention on the Elimination of All Forms of Discrimination Against Women (and the UN Declaration on the Elimination of Violence Against Women), the UN Commission on the Status of Women has helped develop a range of international laws governing certain kinds of child labour – labour which is sadly on the increase, especially among girls.

The key to development

As an illustration of disadvantage from the beginning, the UNICEF information sheet 'Women and Girls – The Key to Development' describes how in many countries more boys than girls survive the difficult first five years of life although girls are born stronger and with a longer life expectancy.

> **The 1989 Convention on the Rights of the Child proclaims the right to equality between boys and girls, yet girls still suffer various kinds of deprivation**

Bias against girls in health care has been documented in several studies in developing countries. More boys are immunised and treated by hospitals than girls and infant and toddler girls in many countries enjoy less nutritious food (including shorter breast-feeding).

Under article 24 of the Convention on the Rights of the Child, equal access to health care for boys and girls is required, but the main obstacle is not the inadequate provision of services; it is parental choice and behaviour.

In many cultures adolescent girls are found husbands by their parents so that they arrive at marriage without the education that would have given them knowledge of the require-ments for healthy reproduction, and with bodies inadequately developed for the trials of pregnancy and childbirth. Every hazard facing the young child is heightened by a mother's youth and ignorance.

In some countries the passage from girlhood to womanhood is marked by rituals which can be harmful, like female circumcision. Practices such as genital mutilation are a violation of girls' human rights and are condemned by the Convention on the Rights of the Child. Also of great concern is the abortion of unwanted female foetuses and the high incidence of girl infanticide.

Education

Although there has been a dramatic increase in the proportion of educated children in the past twenty years, boys have fared much better than girls.

High on the list of priorities after the World Conference on Education for All in 1990 were: closing the literacy gap between women and men by the year 2000; and making sure that all children, girls as well as boys, at least finish primary school.

The gender disparity widens during the secondary school phase. Education is the most important vehicle for ensuring women's equal access to knowledge, skills, jobs and participation in society.

The 1990 World Summit for Children underlined the urgent situation of the girl child, declaring that 'girls must be given equal treatment and opportunities from the very beginning.'

Legislation and employment

Even in states that have passed progressive laws affecting women and girls, the civil law is widely ignored in favour of men. Women lack effective legal protection in both the public and private spheres of life. There is also an urgent need to achieve equality in the workplace, with equal pay for equal work; furthermore, a sustained effort is required to measure and evaluate unremunerated work of a domestic nature and agricultural work.

Rural poverty

It is estimated that about sixty per cent of the world's one billion rural poor are female, and female-headed households are increasing worldwide with divorced, widowed or single women falling deeper into poverty.

ACWW statement

'*From Invisibility to Official Recognition*', ACWW's statement to the preparatory meeting for the UN Conference on Women in Beijing, pinpoints the twin issues of:
- the value of women's unpaid work and their contribution to the wealth of society; and
- the potential and strategic importance of the girl child.

To ensure the future stability of families and society, ACWW believes that the well-being and potential of the girl child must be enhanced through effective measures taken by national governments.

Beijing workshop

ACWW held a workshop at the NGO Forum in Beijing in collaboration with other organisations, opened by World President Lyndsay Hacket-Pain introducing the theme, '*The Potential and Strategic Importance of the Girl Child*'. At Beijing and beyond, by incorporating this perspective into its 'women in development' concerns, ACWW's aim is to become a strong advocate for the girl child.

Girlhood: A perilous path

Prebirth
Tests that tell the gender of the foetus may be used to de-select girls and abort them.

Birth
An unwanted girl baby may be killed at birth in parts of Asia, or allowed to die when she falls ill.

Infancy
Girls are more resilient than boys, but shorter breastfeeding and less nurture reduce their chances.

Early childhood (age 1-5)
Less food and fewer visits to the health clinic make a girl more susceptible to sickness and stunted growth.

Childhood (age 6-12)
A heavy load of domestic duties – sibling care, cleaning, cooking, water-carrying, minding the house – robs girls of childhood and education.

Adolescence
Girls who are unschooled and an economic burden are married off at an early age, by arrangement and sometimes for cash.

Teenage motherhood
Babies born to girls under 18 are often born too early and are too small. A quarter of the 500,000 women who die annually from maternity are teenage girls.

It is hoped that the Beijing Conference will lead to a significant breakthrough in approaches to women's development and to an improvement in women's status by ending discrimination against the girl child.

Helping governments keep their promises

The International Conference on Population and Development (ICPD) in Cairo produced one of the most progressive agendas for change to come out of any UN conference, redefining population programmes and urging alternative solutions.

However, translating its agenda into action will require careful and sustained monitoring of government policy commitments as well as focused advocacy with international and donor agencies.

Women's groups believe the Cairo accomplishments must be linked to other, related UN conferences, especially the March Social Summit in Copenhagen and the Women's Conference in Beijing, to ensure that ICPD goals are kept in sight.

In New York this spring, at the daily NGO Women's Caucus at the final UN PrepCom for Beijing, representatives from nearly 180 countries discussed many of these concerns and their growing responsibilities in the post-Cairo era. They agreed that, on the whole, the ICPD Programme of Action had greatly improved women's negotiating positions vis-a-vis their governments. Their key concern was how to use the Cairo declarations to compel governmental and international agencies to reorder priorities so that programmes related to women's reproductive health could be implemented.

The good news is that major networks are actively engaged in making Cairo concepts a reality and disseminating information regularly.

● The above is an extract from *News & Views*, Women's Environment & Development Organisation.
© *Countrywoman*
October/December, 1995

INDEX

benefits (State)
    and equal opportunities 2-3, 26, 28
boys
    self-esteem of 13 and 14 year old 32
    views of girls 33
bullying, female 34, 35

childcare
    and the 'care deficit' 30-1
    and dual-career couples 10-11
    equal responsibilities of fathers 21-2

Demos 30, 34, 35
discrimination *see* sex discrimination

earnings *see* pay
economic growth, and progress on sex equality 26
education
    and equal opportunities 2, 26, 28, 36-7
    girls compared with boys 32
    and young women 30
employment
    changing patterns of 25, 26
    and dual-career couples 10-11
    family-friendly policies 21, 22, 28
    history of women's 4-5
    inequalities in 2, 12-13, 20, 24
    patterns of men 8, 15
    patterns of women 13, 14, 15, 24, 30
        in the European Union 9, 12, 15
    progress on equality in 26
    sex discrimination in 1, 8
    women's economic activity rates 29
equal opportunities
    and education 2, 26, 28, 36-7
    and health care 28, 36, 37
    and sport 3
    and welfare benefits 2-3, 26, 28
    in the workplace 1-29
Equal Opportunities Commission (EOC) 2-3, 8, 25
    Equality Agenda for pay 13
    and Fair Play 27
    National Agenda for Action 3, 24, 28-9
    and sexual harassment 16-20
    Women and Men in Britain 26

equal pay 6, 12, 13, 28
equal value, work of 1, 13
European Union (EU), and women in employment 9, 12, 15

Fair Play 27
Fawcett Society 23
feminism
    and families 11, 22
    media image of 25

girls
    self-esteem of 13 and 14 year old 32
    and sport 3
    status of girl children 36-7
    views of boys 33
    and violence 34-5

health care 28, 36, 37
health problems 29, 35
housework, and men 14, 23

industrial tribunals, and sexual harassment cases 17, 19-20

life expectancy of women 14

maternity leave/rights 6, 26, 28
men
    employment patterns 8, 15
    and housework 14, 23
    pay compared with women 5, 8, 10, 12, 13, 14, 15, 31
    and sex discrimination 8, 25
    and unemployment 9, 24, 29
    and women's work 4
    and workplace inequality 20
minimum wages 12
mothers
    as single parents 22, 24, 29
    teenage motherhood 37
    working 10-11, 23, 24, 29

parents
    dual-career couples as 10-11
Parliament, representation of women in 4, 13
part-time workers
    discrimination against 1
    equal status for 26
    job opportunities 25
    pay 25
    and pensions 3
    women as 10, 11, 13, 15, 20, 31

pay
    equal 6, 12, 13, 28
    men compared with women 5, 8, 10, 12, 13, 14, 15, 31
pensions, equality in 2-3, 26
poverty, and women 28, 31
professional jobs, women in 4, 14, 24, 31, 35

retirement, equality in 2

Scotland, sexual harassment cases 19-20
sex discrimination
    direct and indirect 1
    and men 8, 25
Sex Discrimination Act (1975) 1, 2, 30
sexual harassment 1, 16-20
    dealing with 17-18
    defining 16
suffragette movement 4

trade unions, and women 5, 12
training
    and equal opportunities 26, 28

unemployment, men and women compared 9, 24, 29

wages, minimum 12
women
    economic activity rate for 29
    employment patterns 13, 14, 15, 24, 30
        by type of occupation 24
        in the European Union 9, 12, 15
    government policies desired by 6-7
    history of women's work 4-5
    leisure activities 14, 24
    life expectancy 14
    media portrayal of 28
    in 'men's jobs' 2
    pay compared with men 5, 8, 10, 12, 13, 14, 15, 31
    and politics 4, 13, 24
    in top jobs 2, 14
    and unemployment 9, 24, 29
    and violent crime 34, 35
    young women 30-1
    see also mothers

young people 30-7

ADDITIONAL RESOURCES

You might like to contact the following organisations for further information. Due to the increasing cost of postage, many organisations cannot respond to enquiries unless they receive a stamped, addressed envelope.

Advisory, Conciliation and Arbitration Service (ACAS)
23 Wilton Street
London SW1X 7AZ
Tel: 0171 210 3613
Fax: 0171 210 3708

Department for Education & Employment
Sex Equality Branch
Room 400c
Caxton House
Tothill Street
London SW1H 9NF
Tel: 0171 273 5325

Produces useful publications including *The best of both worlds – a guide to flexible working*. Available free from Cambertown Ltd
Tel: 01709 888688

Equal Opportunities Commission
Overseas House
Quay Street
Manchester M3 3HN
Tel: 0161 833 9244
Fax: 0161 835 1657

Deals with sex discrimination. They provide legal advice and produce a wide range of publications (some free).

Equal Opportunities Commission for Northern Ireland
Chamber of Commerce House
22 Great Victoria Street
Belfast BT2 7BA
Northern Ireland
Tel: 01232 242752
Fax: 01232 331047

Equal Opportunities Commission – Scotland
Stock Exchange House
7 Nelson Mandela Place
Glasgow G2 1QW
Scotland
Tel: 0141 248 5833
Fax: 0141 248 5834

Equal Opportunities Commission – Wales

Caerwys House
Windsor Lane
Cardiff CF1 1LB
Tel: 01222 343552
Fax: 01222 641 079

Fawcett Society
46 Harleyford Road
London SE11 5AY
Tel: 0171 628 4441

Aims to influence parliament and public opinion to accept equal status for women in the home and public life, and equal educational and job opportunities. Produces *Towards Equality*, a quarterly publication. To subscribe, send £25:00 to Fawcett Society, Free-post FE6903, London EC2B 2JD

Low Pay Unit
37-29 Amwell Street
London EC1R 1UN
Tel: 0171 713 7616
Fax: 0171 713 7581

Investigates low pay, poverty and related issues. Produces newsletters and reports.

National Alliance of Women's Organisations (NAWO)
279-281 Whitechapel Road
London E1 1BY
Tel: 0171 247 7052

To eliminate all forms of discrimination. Policy work on issues of importance to women i.e. representation in the media, rural issues, black and ethnic minorities and education etc. Produces publications

National Council of Women of Great Britain
36 Danbury Street
London N1 8JU
Tel: 0171 354 2395
Fax: 0171 354 9214

Works towards the removal of discrimination against women. Produces publications.

Scottish Trades Union Congress
Woodlands Terrace
Glasgow G3 6ED
Tel: 0141 332 2045

Trades Union Congress (TUC)
Congress House
23-28 Great Russell Street
London WC1B 3LS
Tel: 0171 636 4030

Women's Educational Training Trust (WETT)
Blackburn House
Hope Street
Liverpool L1 9JB
Tel: 0151 709 4356
Fax: 0151 709 8293

Establishes and promotes equal opportunities in education and training. Encourages women into non–traditional jobs. Produces publications.

Women's Health
52-54 Featherstone Street
London EC1Y 8RT
Tel: 0171 251 6580

Provides a variety of resources on many aspects of women's health.

Women's International League for Peace and Freedom (British Section)
157 Lyndhurst Road
Worthing
Sussex BN11 2DG
Tel: 01903 205161

Aims for removal of discrimination on grounds of sex, race or creed.

Women's National Commission
Level 4, Caxton House
Tothill Street
London SW1H 9NF
Tel: 0171 273 5486

Independent advisory committee to government which aims to ensure that women's views are heard and considered. Produces publications.

ACKNOWLEDGEMENTS

The publisher is grateful for permission to reproduce the following material.

While every care has been taken to trace and acknowledge copyright, the publisher tenders its apology for any accidental infringement or where copyright has proved untraceable. The publisher would be pleased to come to a suitable arrangement in any such case with the rightful owner.

Chapter One: Work and equality

The Sex Discrimination Act, © Reproduced with the kind permission of Her Majesty's Stationery Office HMSO, January 1996, *Challenging inequalities between men and women*, © Equal Opportunities Commission, *The long struggle for equality*, © The Guardian, June 1995, *Work: progress on equality but still lagging over pay*, © The Telegraph plc, London 1995, *Asking for it*, © everywoman, March 1996, *Official: men finally losing the sex war*, © The Times Newspapers Ltd, May 1996, *Women and men at work*, © CREW, 1995, *A time for women*, © The Guardian, April 1996, *Wage determination and sex segregation in the labour market*, © CREW, 1995, *The inequality gap*, © Equal Opportunities Commission, *Women's lot is still less pay, more work*, © The Guardian, August 1995, *Employment and key facts on women*, © Reproduced with the kind permission of Her Majesty's Stationery Office HMSO, May 1996, *What is sexual harassment?*, © Equal Opportunities Commission, *What can you do if you are sexually harassed?*, © Equal Opportunities Commission, *Sexual harassment cases in Scotland*, © Equal Opportunities Commission, *Men now victims of workplace inequality*, © The Telegraph plc, London 1996, *Whatever happened to Pa?*, © The Guardian, April 1996, *Stereotyping and prejudices*, © Reproduced with the kind permission of Her Majesty's Stationery Office HMSO, July 1995, *Helping with the housework*, © Fawcett Society, Summer 1996, *A woman's place is in the wider world*, © The Telegraph plc, London 1995, *Fem and us*, © The Guardian, April 1996, *The future challenges*, © Equal Opportunities Commission, *Fair Play . . .*, © Equal Opportunities Commission, *In pursuit of equality*, Women's National Commission, *Women's participation in the labour market*, © Reproduced with the kind permission of Her Majesty's Stationery Office HMSO.

Chapter Two: Young people and equality

The post-equality generation, © Fawcett Society, 1996, *Division of Household tasks*, © MORI, Whirlpool Foundation, *Expectations for the future*, © Health Education Authority, 1996, *Boys' and girls' views of each other*, © Health Education Authority, 1996, *Girls get violent*, © The Independent, May 1996, *The girl child*, © Countrywoman, October/December 1995.

Photographs and Illustrations

Pages 1, 4, 6, 14, 21, 26: Ken Pyne, pages 8, 19: Andrew Smith / Folio Collective, pages 17, 23: Katherine Fleming / Folio Collective, page 34: Anthony Haythornthwaite / Folio Collective.

Craig Donnellan
Cambridge
September, 1996